objects

OF

OUR

desire

When the Body Speaks

Mahler and Kohut

The Birth of Hatred

The Internal Mother

Intimacy and Infidelity

The Seasons of Life

The Seed of Madness

The Colors of Childhood

Brothers and Sisters

Thicker than Blood

Does God Help?

Three Faces of Mourning

Mental Zoo

Cultural Zoo

The Language of Emotions

Real and Imaginary Fathers

Freud along the Ganges

Severe Personality Disorders

The Crescent and the Couch

EXPLORING

OUR

INTIMATE CONNECTIONS

WITH THE THINGS

AROUND US

HARMONY BOOKS
NEW YORK

objects

OF

OUR

desire

SALMAN AKHTAR, M.D.

Grateful acknowledgment is made to Viking Penguin for permission to reprint the poem "Things," translated by Stephen Kessler. Copyright © 1999 by Maria Kodama. Translation copyright © 1999 by Stephen Kessler. From *Selected Poems* by Jorge Luis Borges, edited by Alexander Coleman. Reprinted by permission of Viking Penguin, a division of Penguin Group (USA) Inc.

Published in the United States by Harmony Books,
an imprint of the Crown Publishing Group, a division
of Random House, Inc., New York.
www.crownpublishing.com

Harmony Books is a registered trademark and the Harmony
Books colophon is a trademark of Random House, Inc.

Library of Congress Cataloging-in-Publication Data
Akhtar, Salman, 1946–
Objects of our desire : exploring our intimate connections with
the things around us / Salman Akhtar.—1st ed.
Includes bibliographical references.
1. Transitional objects (Psychology)   I. Title.
BF175.5.T73A38   2005
155.9'1—dc22   2005003389

ISBN 1-4000-5444-3

Printed in the United States of America

DESIGN BY ELINA D. NUDELMAN

10   9   8   7   6   5   4   3   2   1

First Edition

to my mother's gramophone

contents

11   PROLOGUE: GANDHI'S PAPER CLIP

everything

17   ACQUIRING AND USING THINGS

29   COLLECTING AND HOARDING THINGS

something

53   NOSTALGIC THINGS

75   SACRED THINGS

93   SEXY THINGS

CONTENTS

117   HYBRID THINGS

137   FAKE THINGS

nothing

157   MISPLACING, LOSING, AND
      LETTING GO OF THINGS

177   BECOMING A THING

199   EPILOGUE: A LITTLE SILVER BOX
      INSIDE THE PARROT'S HEART

203   NOTES

217   ACKNOWLEDGMENTS

220   INDEX

prologue: gandhi's paper clip

During the last years of his life, Gandhi was well-known around the world. In India, he was nearly worshipped. People called him "Bapu," an endearing term for father. Everyone wanted to see him. Hundreds waited in front of his home merely to catch a glimpse of him. Ever inventive, Gandhi found a way to accommodate them by doing his paperwork and responding to his correspondence while sitting in his front yard. His secretary would read aloud the mail that had arrived and Gandhi would dictate a few lines to him in response. A cordon was erected around the space where Gandhi worked with his secretary. People passed the area quietly, gazing at him in awe, many bowing down to touch the ground where he had walked.

One day the secretary opened an envelope. Two sheets of paper, attached to each other by a paper clip, came out. He began to read the letter, gasped, and became silent. Quickly, he crumpled the sheets of paper and threw them in the wastebasket. Gandhi asked him the reason for this and was told that the letter contained obscenities directed at him. The secretary suggested that they move on to the next piece of mail, but Gandhi insisted upon reading the letter himself. Once he had finished, he took the paper clip out and threw the two sheets of paper away. His secretary was amazed that he did not look upset at all. "Bapu, has the hatred in this letter not hurt you?" Gandhi smiled and said that he was not affected because he was certain that the epithets and curses in the letter had no application to him at all. He added that the man who wrote the letter perhaps knew this too and, to make up for his assault, had sent along the gift of a paper clip. It was as important to not let the hatred contaminate oneself as it was to enjoy the gift of this paper clip.

Did this episode actually happen or is it folklore? Did the letter writer unconsciously intend what Gandhi attributed to him? Was Gandhi being genuinely forgiving or was it a clever ploy to salvage an embarrassing social situation? These questions are certainly worthwhile. However, to my mind, the most important question is whether we can recognize that in the midst of the inevitable suffering of life, solace and even joy often come to us in the form, so to speak, of a paper clip.

This book is a celebration of such "paper clips" and, indeed, of all objects, big or little, that make our lives safe, interesting, pleasant—and meaningful.

everything

acquiring and using things

Look around. What do you see?

Lamps, tables, chairs, flower vases, paintings, pillows, newspapers, magazines, books? Or, if you happen to be in your kitchen, perhaps your eyes move from the refrigerator to the stove and from the microwave to the dishwasher and finally to the pots and pans in the sink. If you aren't at home but at a bus stop or an airport, you can hardly avoid noticing the large number of things that are—or, shall we say, have become—part of our lives and inhabit all the nooks and crannies of our existence. Things play an important role in how we navigate the world, communicate with one an-other, connect with our pasts, and express our

desires. The emotional significance of physical ob‚
jects is unmistakably evident all around us.

You don't believe me?

Notice the inviting contours of that sofa, the
glint of a knife's edge, the sparkle of a diamond ring.
Feel the softness of the pashmina around that
woman's milky shoulders. Look at the majesty of a
large jet plane. Take in the somberness of a grave‚
stone. Put on an old pair of shoes. Clutch a warm
mug of freshly brewed coffee. Sit on a rocking chair.
Feel the sumptuous leather seats of a new car.

We are surrounded by things. We are involved
with them, indebted to them. We speak to things
and things speak to us. To say that we are interde‚
pendent is banal. Let us be courageous. Let us ad‚
mit it: we are lovers.

And, like lovers, we are inseparable, even though
we are often unable to express our love of things in
words. Here poets come to our rescue. In his poem
"Ode to Things," the great Chilean poet Pablo Ne‚
ruda openly voices his attachment to and his de‚
light in the emotional gifts of the material world:

I pause in houses,
streets and
elevators,
touching things,

identifying objects
that I secretly covet;
this one because it rings,
that one because
it's as soft
as the softness of a woman's hip,
that one there for its deep-sea color,
and that one for its velvet feel.

Even in less joyous forms, things form an integral part of our lives. We constantly discover, or as Freud would have it, rediscover them. Things affect our emotions and impact upon our thoughts. The arrival of a dozen roses from a lover or a letter from a grandchild makes our day. And we express our emotions, or innermost selves, with their help. Welling with love, we offer gifts, tokens of our affection. Feeling sad, we may reach for an old photo album that offers us friendly faces and memories of good times. Bitter and enraged, we give vent to our suppressed emotions by reading a book about a serial killer and vicariously identifying with his cruel acts. Such "conversation" between us and things is of course affected by our cultural heritage, by our gender, by our knowing and unknowing emulation of (or rebellion against) our parents, by our economic status, and by the value we place on material acquisitions, but it is universal. As such, we must first ask ourselves a truly basic question:

Why do we need things?

Things satisfy all sorts of physical and emotional needs in us. To begin with, they offer us "instru-mental" help. We enlist their prowess to accom-plish the tasks of daily living. We use cars, planes, trains, and boats for travel; clocks and watches for knowing time; knives to cut; spoons to feed our-selves with; chairs to sit upon; and so on. Actually, if we are honest and humble, we will acknowledge that our very survival depends upon things. As *naked apes,* which is what the ethologist Desmond Morris called human beings, we are hardly capable of surviving the harshness of nature alone. Inani-mate objects come to our aid and save our lives.

We need enclosed spaces—made of "things"—to live, clothes to cover our vulnerable furless skin, artificial means to travel long distances, and all sorts of cooking utensils to render digestible what we devour. Our dependence upon things is not merely life-saving and life-enhancing, it confers upon us the dignity of our human status as well. Try walking out of your house naked on the street and you will immediately bow to the profound role such plebian things as clothes silently play in your acceptance by society. It is a pity that the discourse on the Garden of Eden waxes eloquently about God's injunctions, Adam, Eve, the forbidden fruit, and even the wicked serpent but pays little attention to the poor fig leaf, the primordial hint of the human civilization to come.

The progression from that "original garment" to haute couture is mirrored in the transitions from wooden spears to Kalashnikovs, from flickering oil lamps to incandescent lightbulbs, and from horse-drawn carriages to gas-guzzling SUVs. Necessity, the mother of invention, has indeed turned out to be a fertile woman. As a result, the world is full of useful things that, in Borges's words, "serve us like slaves who never say a word."

At the same time, it is obvious that our dependence upon things has something more than their utilitarian value at its base. From birth till death, we draw all sorts of emotional sustenance from them.

Things and our emotional growth

At the beginning of our lives, man, animal, and things are all the same to us. Differentiation between them develops gradually. Over time, we begin to react differently to human and non-human objects. Upon seeing our mothers, we give a "social response," but to a toy we give an "acquisitive response." The former consists of smiling, chuckling, and reaching out to a person. The latter consists of deliberate movements of arms and hands to grasp an object. By six months of age, we no longer accept an inanimate object in lieu of a person. And yet we continue to think of objects as being alive. Until we are six or seven, we think that the sun and the moon move because they *want* to and toys have feelings that must be considered.

Meanwhile, the game of peekaboo teaches us that just because we can no longer see an object, it has not actually disappeared. Over time, our understanding of this concept shapes our understanding of the entire world of things. A tree, we learn, will remain a tree; a house, a house.

During this time, which spans from about six months to eighteen months of age, we are also beginning to psychologically separate from our mothers. To handle the resulting feelings of loneliness, we find our first real possession, usually a teddy bear or a blanket. Affectionately cuddled, it provides a sense of comfort and safety. Donald Winnicott, the British pediatrician turned psychoanalyst, emphasizes that the child's teddy bear or blanket helps create the experiential realm be-

tween the inner world and external reality. A pos‹
session of this sort is tangible, but its importance
lies in the feelings it produces, not in its actual use.
As a result, such an object becomes the harbinger
of the capacity to experience the world on a
metaphorical level. Reality no longer appears jux‹
taposed to unreality; emotions that bridge the two
in subtle and intangible ways begin to be experi‹
enced. With further development, such "interme‹
diate area of experience" allows for the enjoyment
of poetry, music, fiction, and movies (all being nei‹
ther real nor not real; intangible yet perceived).

The fact that potential groundwork for creative
thinking is laid by the early interplay between the
mind and its physical surround is well captured in
a 1926 poem by Julian Huxley:

> The world of things entered in your infant
>   mind
> To populate that crystal cabinet.
> Within its walls the strangest partners met.
> And things turned thoughts did propagate their
>   kind.
> For, once within, corporeal fact could find
> A spirit. Fact and you in mutual debt
> Built there your little microcosm—which yet
> Had hugest tasks to its small self assigned.

Still later in childhood, we notice how our bodies are either the same or different from our parents'. We notice gender roles as well, and physical
objects help us to define ourselves. Little girls play
dress-up with their mother's lipstick and jewelry,
while little boys want to try on their father's shoes
and raincoat. Not only do we learn the ability of
objects to help create who we are—or who we
want to be—but we feel a thrill from using
"adult" objects. As clothing begins to help shape
our personal identity, other objects help develop
our social lives. Board games, sports equipment,
video games, and other toys help us play with
others and are the first ways in which we interact
with our peers and begin to form friendships.

Puberty brings on an uncompromising need to
forge our identities, and objects are critical to this
undertaking. At this point, we almost become a
thing ourselves, as how we look—our clothes,
hair, makeup, tattoos—becomes the most important way we announce who we are and what we
believe. Our rooms also take on profound importance as refuges and as another way to announce
ourselves through the posters, banners, photos,
and souvenirs we stock them with. Inanimate
objects function in three different ways: first, as a
reflection of our changing bodies (razors, bras,

sanitary napkins, zit creams); next, from tongue rings to ripped jeans, they are a way to rebel against our parents; finally, there are the physical objects that help us disengage from our childhood self-image and are pathways to our future—the CD collection, the guitar, the posters and art that adorn the walls. These objects testify to our growing reliance on the value of our peers rather than our parents. As we did when we were children playing dress-up, we try on a variety of roles until we find the ones that best fit and we mature.

As we move out on our own, go to college, find jobs, and develop mature romantic relationships, the nature and meaning of the objects of importance change. For the first time, we can set our sights higher: on furniture, appliances, a car, an apartment, a home. To be sure, socioeconomic and cultural variables affect the extent to which we acquire such possessions, but the move into adulthood invariably involves a material dimension. Establishing a home of our own usually involves a wide array of things: stereo systems, microwave ovens, televisions, tables, forks and knives, couches and bookcases. The rituals of courtship, engagement, and marriage or commitment also have an extensive material component. The period of courtship, regardless of whether it results in marriage, is especially marked by the acquisition of new material objects. These include gifts for the beloved, additions to one's own wardrobe, and things one buys together as a couple.

This last category of things grows with leaps and bounds once we enter a marital relationship. Still later, raising children forces us to come into contact with our childhood objects again—stroller, high chair, tricycle, board games—an encounter that can have significant replenishing effects for our adult selves. Playing with our children's toys brings back happy memories of a bygone era. The pleasure is akin to the one felt upon meeting an old friend after a long time. It makes us smile, reminisce, and synthesize different phases of life in a harmonious way.

A time to "downsize"

Middle age changes our relationship to physical objects in enriching as well as unsettling ways. By now, most of us have acquired a lot of things. In addition to the purely useful—appliances, clothing, et cetera—we've acquired a substantial cache of sentimental items: family photographs, souvenirs from past vacations, mementos from old friends, legacies from lost loved ones. These objects not only connect us to our history but also bond us to our loved ones. These items hold our memories and are the glue that holds us together, especially to our spouses. At this stage, financial security and more time for self-reflection may inspire the purchase of things previously unavailable to us or considered only dreams: a sports car, fine china, diamonds, a second home.

Gradually, however, we reach the limits of what we can acquire. We begin to sense the limits of our achievements, creativity, and most important, of our life itself. Bodily changes, children moving on, and parents passing away cause further strain on our minds. Time now enters the psychic domain in a powerful way. Death no longer remains merely a topic for courses in a community college. Less of life appears to be left, more spent.

As we age further, toward retirement and beyond, most of us become aware that material possessions are ephemeral. Novel and desirable at first, they gradually lose their glitter. A deep and satisfying experience of life hardly emanates from what we have acquired; it comes from the love we have given and received. Such knowledge alters our relationship to things. As a result, we enter into a gradual downsizing of material life, buying less but enjoying what we have more, and considering the fate of our possessions after we are gone. We write wills, think privately about our graves or the fate of our ashes.

Toward the end

In the waning years of life, our relationship with things returns to one of dependence. We rely on canes, wheelchairs, diapers, pillboxes, and dentures for our safety and well-being. Ultimately, we may find ourselves relying on machines for our existence. The end forces us to say good-bye to the world of things. Everything has to go. Or is it that we go away and "things" remain?

Throughout our lives, we need "things" not only for their actual usefulness but for their emotional value to us as well. Things help us express ourselves. An expensive car lets others know that we have "arrived," and a lovingly kept heirloom informs them of our affection for our ancestors. Things also contribute to our identity. Someone looking at our possessions can surmise if we are art lovers, Civil War buffs, bibliophiles, and so on. And the emotional purposes served by things keep changing as our lives unfold. At one point their role is clear, while at another point it is clouded in mystery. Some emotional purposes served by things are obvious, others hidden. An encounter with a serious collector drives this last point home.

collecting and
hoarding things

Sigmund Freud's office was filled with books and antiquities. Randolph Hearst's ostentatious collection still fills an entire castle in San Luis Obispo, California. On a far less grand level, my thirty-year-old son has carefully preserved all his childhood toys; snug in their original packages, they occupy a significant portion of the storage space in our attic. And my secretary's brother, David, filled the back of his bedroom door with rock-band stickers during his teenage years and took the door with him (!) when he moved out of the family home. These might be extreme illustrations, but the tendency to collect they exemplify is far from uncommon.

Terry Kovel, who writes the *Kovels' Antiques*

and Collectibles Price Guide books with her husband, Ralph, is fond of saying, "One out of three people collects." In fact, most people have a bit of the collector in them even if it goes unrecognized. Men who keep buying gadgets and golf clubs and women who have a passion for shoes clearly collect things but are hardly known as "collectors." It is the individual who ardently accumulates a sizable number of a specific thing who is called a "collector." Why do people collect? What drives them to spend time and money in order to enhance their collection? What intoxicating pleasure do they derive from collecting despite the hardships that often come with this hobby?

But wait, do we really know what a collection is? How does it differ from clutter? Is one person's clutter another person's collection, and vice versa? Or can the two types of accumulations be distinguished?

Collection versus clutter

To understand the collector, first we must define a "collection," particularly as it differs from clutter. Clutter consists of things (e.g., unopened junk mail, old newspapers, empty beer bottles in the garage) that are not specifically valued by their owner, while a collection consists of objects that are lovingly accumulated. More important, clutter results from an inability to discard things, while a collection results from an active pursuit of objects. Clutter originates from passivity (we're too lazy to discard the items we no longer need) or insecurity (we feel safe saving everything in case we need it at some future date). A collection, in contrast, involves activity. A collection does not "happen" by itself; it is the end product of laborious pursuit. Collectors go to all lengths to obtain the objects they love. Wandering around flea markets, surfing the Internet, visiting specifically geared conventions, and showing up at estate auctions are all part of the industriousness a collector shows.

Money also gets involved in this pursuit. Collectors often spend considerable amounts of money to obtain a particular item that catches their fancy. And, conversely, collections themselves can fetch large sums of money upon being sold. Clutter has no such value. Yet another difference between clutter and a collection is that the former is quantitative and the latter qualitative. Indeed, collectors can be quite discerning and do not acquire everything that belongs to the category of objects they collect. For example, a person who collects wristwatches or pens does not buy every watch or pen he comes across. Instead, he carefully selects one that is made in a particular era or country, or one that has some special, desirable feature. The clutterer, in contrast, lets any and everything gather around himself.

Some overlap between clutter and collection does, however, exist. For instance, a collection might arise out of clutter. Something discovered in the heap may spark the desire to actively collect that particular object. Yesterday's clutter gives birth to today's collection. The reverse can also happen. Over time, the desire to collect can become a compulsion, an inner tyranny of sorts. When this happens, collecting just one type of object—say, ceramic vases or matchbooks—is no longer satisfying. The collector begins to collect more and more things, and what was originally a hobby threatens to turn into an addiction.

My friends Naresh and Bubble Julka frequently travel abroad and some years ago began collecting little clocks from all over the world. Soon they moved on to blue china and then to Egyptian figurines, Russian dolls, Turkish plates, and a few other objects that I, frankly, fail to even remember. Their house has so many display cases and curio cabinets holding these "collections" that there is hardly any place to walk. The mantelpiece is overflowing with objects, and if you are having a drink in their living room, you will find it hard to put it down on the end table. The terrain of their home is already "populated" by inanimate dignitaries from this or that country.

Is this collection or clutter? Collecting one particular object (e.g., stamps, coins, nail clippers) belongs to the category of collection. Collecting multiple objects, unless it is in the hands of some truly dedicated individual, begins to blur boundaries between collection and clutter. The kind of adoring attention that one lavishes upon a collection of single objects is difficult to give to collections of multiple objects. (Think of it as the difference between a happy marriage and wild promiscuity!) Under these circumstances, activity begins to be replaced by passivity. The "desire to collect" is gradually transformed into the "inability to not collect." Even in less-driven instances, an inner passivity or a poetic surrender develops in regard to the pressure to collect. We are left to marvel at man's hunger for physical objects.

Usual and unusual objects for collection

Although what people collect might be different, the desire to collect is universal. People all over the world are inclined to this passion and it is impossible to list all the things that they collect. The possibilities go from A almost to Z: art deco objects, baskets and bottles, carpets and comic books, dolls and dollhouses, electronic gadgets, Fiestaware and fishing lures, glass (Depression-era glass, Fenton glass, glass figurines, pressed glass, shot glasses, tumblers, and so on) and G.I. Joe figures, harmonicas and hockey cards, Indian trade relics, jewelry, kitchenware, law enforcement memorabilia, origami, Pez dispensers and plates and purses, quilts, records, sports memorabilia and stamps, teddy bears and tobacco-related artifacts (cigarette lighters, cigarette holders, ashtrays, snuffboxes, cigar cutters, cigar boxes, pipes, parts of pipes . . . you get the idea), and watches.

Clearly people collect all sorts of imaginable and unimaginable things. Collections of the rich and famous are most well-known, like Freud's collection of Greek and Egyptian antiquities, Prince Rainier's stamp albums, Paul Getty's treasury of art and antiques, Albert Barnes's accumulation of great Impressionist paintings, and even Jay Leno's bevy of antique cars and motorcycles. Lesser-known individuals have also amassed collections that are unique and fascinating:

- Ed Brassard (of the United States) has amassed 3,159,119 matchbook covers.

- Peter Broker (of Germany) has a collection of 8,131 different full beer bottles from 110 countries.

- Andre Ludwick (of South Africa) has collected 505 different nail clippers.

- Antoine Secco (of France) has collected more than 26,800 fruit stickers.

- Raghav Somani (of India) has a collection of 469 airline tags from 115 worldwide airlines.

- Niek Vermeulen (of Holland) has 3,240 airline sickness bags from 740 different airlines.

- Jean-François Vernetti (of Switzerland) has collected 2,915 DO NOT DISTURB signs from hotels in 131 different countries.

But why are all the people on this list of "great" and "famous" collectors of the world men? Is it because women lack the financial resources needed to build collections of expensive items such as art and antiques? Or is it because women tend to gather objects for their utilitarian value (e.g., shoes, purses) and such accumulations do not get recognized as "collections"? Or is it possible that women are naturally less inclined to collect things? My sense is that women do collect things but brag less about their collections and are less driven to become "famous" for their collecting passion. It is also possible that women have been denied fame in the male-dominated writings about collections. Either way, they remain less known as collectors. Few know the names of Alice Fletcher (1838–1923), Helen Roberts (1888–1985), Frances Densmore (1867–1957), and Laura Boulton (1899–1980), and their collections of artifacts from American Indians, Eskimos, and people of the Caribbean Islands remain largely unrecognized. And, in the same vein, Isabella Stuart Gardner (1840–1924) and Peggy Guggenheim (1898–1979), the great collectors of art, also remain less known than, say, Paul Getty or Randolph Hearst.

Our emotional reactions to collections

The range of objects people collect is astonishingly wide and so are our emotional reactions to such collections. We are all familiar with people who collect stamps, coins, matchboxes, toys, key chains, subway tokens, pillboxes, timepieces, and baseball cards. We view such collections as somehow "normal" and even "understandable." We similarly accept collections of teddy bears, dolls, animal figurines, records, pens, thimbles, and even butterflies and insects. We are fascinated and impressed by collections of art, rare books, autographs, Oriental rugs, sculpture, jewelry, and antique cars. We are intrigued when we see people collecting birds' eggs, things made out of camel bones, unopened letters written by those who have died, old suitcases, and discarded fan belts from airplane engines. In contrast, collections of things owned by serial killers, used gum chewed by famous people, road kill, and artificial eyes make us uneasy. And this feeling turns into incred٬ ulous revulsion when we encounter people who collect boys' used underwear and fossilized di٬ nosaur droppings. Such things are related to sex, dirt, feces, violence, and those aspects of life that are barred from the confines of polite discourse. Encountering them in the form of collections, therefore, makes us uncomfortable.

Different collections affect us in different ways. On the surface, this difference seems to emanate from the realm of aesthetics. Presentation plays a large role. Collections that look appealing or beau٬ tiful tend to please us, while those of a more com٬ mon or gruesome nature don't. A collection of colorful postcards evokes pleasure, while a collec٬ tion of nuts and bolts doesn't. A collection of Bel٬ gian cut glass is generally found more appealing than one of belt buckles from New Mexico.

However, size also affects our emotional re٬ sponse to a collection. Karl Marx's dictum that quantity sooner or later becomes quality seems to apply here. For example, a collection of eight ciga٬ rette lighters won't impress anyone, but a set of eighty or eight hundred would create a stir. Eight thousand would create a sensation. In this case, size matters.

It seems natural that our emotional reaction to a collection of things depends upon its aesthetic appeal to us as well as upon its sheer magnitude. However, our like or dislike is also determined by certain moral judgments that we make. We "approve" of some collections and "disapprove" of others. Coffee mugs and inkwells are acceptable to us, dirty underwear and used hearing aids are not. Bottle caps are okay, navel fluff is not. Toy soldiers are fine, surprising objects found in dog feces are not. Most of us "accept" a collection of pencil sharpeners and antique phones but frown upon a collection of condoms and dildos from all around the world. Vegetarians are repulsed by collections of animal skins, while avid huntsmen appreciate them.

Our emotional response to a collection is, in the end, determined by our value systems. For instance, hunters might enjoy going through a hall full of guns, but pacifists would find the experience disconcerting. Of course, collectors themselves are always approving of their indulgence, and have all sorts of conscious and unconscious reasons for the desire to collect.

Why do people collect things?

Some of us appear incapable of discarding things. This is especially true of those who have experienced painful separations during childhood. Now, to say that someone cannot get rid of an old toaster or useless cardboard boxes in the garage because as a child she was traumatically separated from her parents seems preposterous at first glance. However, when we take into account the intricacies of the human mind, the varying levels of awareness that it operates upon, and the fine nuances of symbolism it employs, the connection no longer seems that strange. The pathway is essentially one from distress over gross or subtle childhood losses to a resultant proclivity to cling to people and things, lifelong anxiety over discarding objects, growing clutter, and then the emergence of a collection as the last step in this chain of events.

Atiya Nasser, an Egyptian-American anthropologist who lives in suburban Virginia and is an avid collector of flower vases, gives voice to this very dynamic. She says, "I am a collector because I had a geographically rootless childhood. While my family was intact and loving, we moved a large number of times. In fact, by the time I was ten years old, I had lived in three different countries.

My collecting passion has to do with the losses I experienced each time we moved—loss of physical space, familiar people, and things. Loss, you know, begets a certain amount of hunger, and this hunger propels one to collect."

While not all collectors are so erudite, at some level they do know that collecting fulfills their deep emotional needs. The desire for permanence is one of them. Those who have had shifting and unstable ground under their feet during childhood especially need stability, and their collections offer them a sense of reassuring warmth.

Collecting also fulfills the ubiquitous human need for exhibitionism and preening. Displaying one's collection to others and looking at it oneself in private, for instance, afford one a well-earned feeling of pride. One feels worthwhile, good, alive: "I collect, therefore I am." Collecting things can thus assuage inner feelings of emptiness, worthlessness, even deadness. In its extreme form, the sense of power derived from possessing a collection can acquire shades of omnipotence. The collector reigning over his empire of inanimate objects begins to feel like a demigod.

The desire for control is an important motivation behind collecting. Collecting things provides us an opportunity to exert control over our world. We can classify, place, move, arrange, rearrange, highlight, name, and even modify the objects of our collection. When it comes to the relationship between our things and us, we are the boss. To those who have felt powerless as children, this sort of dominance over objects can be deeply reward‹ ing. Indeed, clinical experience shows that children chronically betrayed by their parents often turn to animals and things for solace. This shifting of love often leads to a tendency to collect in later life.

Collecting objects is also intricately linked with collecting memories. A collection often starts with a gift given by someone who has parted or died. Looking fondly at a jewel‹studded brooch in the shape of a butterfly, for instance, we might feel im‹ pelled to buy another one like it to make it a pair. We give in to the impulse and experience har‹ mony and happiness. Soon, however, we find the stirrings to repeat this experience and, lo and be‹ hold, in no time, we find ourselves hooked. We are on the way to becoming a collector of butterfly‹ shaped brooches.

Nostalgia is not the only link between collec‹ tion and memory. Another is the desire to deepen a connection to another person by creating mu‹ tual memories. By buying this clock today, a couple brings an item into their life together that at some future point they can look at and recall their mutual pleasure at the purchase. Bringing more clocks home solidifies that experience. As full-fledged collectors, the couple has allowed the clocks to help them create a unique identity. They are the "couple who collects clocks."

Such identity-giving power of the collecting hobby is clear from the stylized designations of various groups of collectors. Of course there are *philatelists* (stamp collectors), *bibliophiles* (book collectors), and *numismatists* (coin collectors), but there are also proud *archtophilists* (collectors of teddy bears), *conchologists* (collectors of shells), *copclephilists* (collectors of key rings), *deltiologists* (collectors of postcards), *lepidopterists* (collectors of butterflies), *plangonophilists* (collectors of dolls), *receptanists* (collectors of recipes), *vecturists* (collectors of subway tokens), and *vexillophilists* (collectors of flags). Interested collectors have had some success in promoting these terms, but, by and large, these "impressive" names are little known outside the circle of devotees, which is usually small in number.

Regardless of whether the object collected is commonplace or obscure, the drive to collect itself arises from a variety of emotional sources. These include protecting oneself from the anxiety about separation and loss, needing power and control, cataloging old memories, creating new memories for the future, and forging a unique sense of personal identity. However, none of this explains why a particular object is chosen by a particular person.

Dalmatians, Beanie Babies, and a bunch of turtles

Why do some people collect stamps and others animal figurines? What makes one man passionate about watches and another about comic books? Certainly there must be a proverbial "method to this madness." After all, both Janet Garrison, a public defender who buys anything that has to do with Dalmatians, and Elizabeth Smith, a librarian who has nearly six hundred Beanie Babies in her apartment, are reasonable people. For Janet, the reason stems from childhood:

> *I grew up sort of lonely. But my mother and father were very nice. They bought a dog when I was about three years old to keep me company. This dog, to which I grew very attached, died when I was twelve or thirteen years old. I was of course very upset. My father took me to a neighborhood animal shelter to see if we could get a puppy for me. And there I saw my first Dalmatian and I immediately fell in love with it. We brought it home. Ever since then, I have had a Dalmatian even though the first one passed away after a few years. I just love Dalmatians. As*

you can see, I have the real dog at home and pictures, calendars, cushions, and porcelain figures of Dalmatians all over my office. I just love them. They are so cute, and you know what? They are really dependent. My dog, Sally, never leaves my side when I am home.

Loss, loneliness, and a poignant need for company are clearly evident in Janet's account. Having discovered a Dalmatian when she was experiencing a painful separation, she's found that her collection of Dalmatian-related items has had a pronounced healing effect upon her. It diminishes her loneliness and keeps her going.

Elizabeth started collecting Beanie Babies under very different circumstances:

Frankly, I am embarrassed to tell anyone that I collect Beanie Babies. I mean, it is a bit silly for a grown-up. Isn't it? . . . Look, it all started with my grandchild, Megan. She was into them and I loved buying them for her. Then a couple of times I bought one that she already had and did not want. So I decided to keep that one for myself. With two or three such Beanie Babies in my possession, I somehow started to want more of them. I got hooked and now I have over six hundred of them.

Loving her grandchild had given her profound joy, and the Beanie Babies collection is a bridge to that bygone era now that her granddaughter has grown out of them. Wistfulness permeates the entire experience.

Looking at the experiences of these two women tells us that the choice of an object to collect is made on highly personal grounds. Even if the deeper issues causing the pressure to collect are similar, the object collected may turn out to be different. Both Janet and Elizabeth were struggling with feelings of loss. Yet their individual life experiences led them to collect different objects.

The opposite happens as well. In other words, people can collect the same thing for entirely different reasons. Take the example of Kelly Devine and Timothy Nevin. Before they met each other, both were avid collectors of turtles. However, they had entirely different motives for doing so. Kelly was very shy and yet worked in a field that necessitated constant interaction with people. Turtles represented her self-image: hard outside, soft inside, quick to withdraw into her shell. Timothy was one of two siblings. His older brother had been regarded as "God's gift to this world" by everyone in the family. This had led Timothy to feel chronically inferior. Then he came across the

Aesop's fable *The Tortoise and the Hare,* which greatly impressed him. He suddenly saw the light. He swore to himself that by hard work and perseverance, one day he would outshine his brother. Turtles (the "tortoise" of the fable) represented his self-image: industrious, plodding, determined to overcome a fortunate rival.

This tells us that similar motivations can lead to different collections and different motivations can lead to similar collections. In other words, we cannot say that all stamp collectors are psychologically alike or all watch collectors have a similar emotional makeup. They might or they might not. We have to hear their individual stories carefully. Only then can we know what underlies their choice of what they collect. While external factors (for instance, the potential of monetary gain) can contribute to the choice of what one collects, the matter is usually of greater subtlety.

Hoarding: the demise of nuance

Far from the indulgent dullness of clutter and the personalized nuance of a collection is the horrifying loss of all subtlety in the case of hoarding. Here man's hunger for things reaches its extreme. The inability to let go of things becomes marked. Emotional emptiness is combated by surrounding oneself with endless layers of material objects. Hoarders grossly exceed the amount of things ordinary pack rats among us can amass. They not only save useless and broken things, they also accumulate quantities of things that are far beyond what anybody can realistically need or ever use. They may gather large quantities of old newspapers and magazines, junk mail, receipts of financial transactions, cans and bottles, old clothes, shoes, vacuum cleaners, plastic containers, cardboard boxes, hangers, broken furniture, and so on. Inability to discard anything, buying excessive quantities of things, and retrieving material from other people's trash combines to create the syndrome of hoarding. Under these circumstances, a home is reduced to a closet. Actual livable space shrinks, fire hazards develop, and entire rooms might become unusable. Neighbors lodge complaints and eviction notices are issued by municipal authorities.

Practically all towns and neighborhoods have their stories of hoarders. Some such individuals end up becoming legends. Franz Lidz of the *New York Times* gives the following nuggets of information:

- In the 1940s, a woman named Theresa Fox was found dead in her New York City apartment. She had more than five hundred cans of evaporated milk stuffed in her mattress and one hundred one-pound bags of coffee stocked in her cupboard. Dozens of loaves of bread were stacked against the kitchen wall and the drawers of her bedroom bureau brimmed with packets of sugar.

- In the 1960s, a Realtor named George Aichele was found dead among heaps of old newspapers, used razor blades, dozens of birdcages, a huge assortment of pipes, and a bunch of musical instruments called zithers.

Across the Atlantic, in 2001, the BBC television show *A Life of Grime* depicted the life of Edmund Trebus. A Polish war veteran, Trebus fought an epic battle against the Municipal Council in North London to remain in his trash-filled house and garden. In the end, he stayed in his house, but the Council succeeded in cleaning up his garden with the use of five large trucks and at the expense of more than $60,000 to the London taxpayers. The house in which Trebus joyfully lived was filled from floor to ceiling with junk and rat-infested rubbish.

None of these tales, however, comes close to the macabre saga of the Collyer brothers. The elderly scions of an affluent New York family, the Collyer brothers lived at the corner of Fifth Avenue and 128th Street in Harlem during the 1940s, and it is there that they were found dead of malnutrition amid a strikingly "opulent" squalor of hoarding. Police, who had broken down the front door, could not walk any farther into the house due to things blocking their way. Gaining access through a second-floor window, they found heaps and heaps of junk, which included the following: fourteen grand pianos, two organs, one clavichord, more than six tons of old newspapers, the chassis of a Model T Ford, a library of fourteen thousand engineering and medical books, an old X-ray machine, the folding top of a horse-drawn carriage, a vast armory of weapons and firearms, three dressmaking dummies, a kerosene stove, six U.S. flags and one Union Jack, an old bicycle, thirty-four bank deposit books, a doll carriage, pin-up-girl photos, a child's chair, gas chandeliers, and a horse's jawbone. All totaled, this junk weighed nearly 180 tons.

Where do we go from here?

This survey has demonstrated that our patterns in acquiring, collecting, and hoarding things reveal much about the way we depend on things for our physical as well as emotional needs. Even our day-to-day interactions with the most common of objects illuminate this relationship, which we often overlook or take for granted. Texture, shape, weight, and color play a role in how we are affected by things and how they affect us. Why do certain objects evoke sadness and others aggression? Why do some make us feel powerful while others create a sense of our insignificance? Why do we regard some things as sacred and others profane? Why do some things stir up a wistful longing for the past while others do not?

something

nostalgic things

It was big, brown, and warm to touch.

That is all I remember of my mother's gramophone. The rest is a bit vague, lost to my past, clouded by regret and longing. The story, I believe, goes more or less like this. When I was a little boy, my mother and I were living in a midsize city in central India. My father had recently moved to Bombay, hoping to find work writing songs for movies. We were to join him once he found a steady job and a suitable place for us to live.

Four hundred miles away in our little apartment, my mother felt lonely without him, and to fill her evenings, she bought a gramophone. She enjoyed the music, but more important, the gramophone and the shiny black 78 rpm records linked her to her husband, the hopeful lyricist miles away. The music, a sonic tether between two cities, sustained her during the long months of his absence.

Then she became sick. She developed a rare connective tissue disease, which, within a few months, caused her to resign from her teaching position at the local university. As she spent more time at home, her reliance on music grew and so did her record collection. She would spend many a long afternoon in bed listening to music, and it became my task to change the records. The gramophone, at first a symbol of her love for my father, now became a powerful link between us. My mother and I both grew very attached to it. It helped us cope with our respective losses: hers, the very real loss of her husband's company and of her health; mine, the loss of an unshakable confidence that my mother would always be with me. I dreaded the thought of losing my mother. Our beloved gramophone filled these gaping holes in both our hearts.

It was big, brown, and warm to touch.

And, you know, as I begin to focus, two other features of it gradually come back to me. The first involves its stylus and the second the manufacturer's emblem on its side. The metallic stylus, round and shiny, had a cutout design that made it look like a little kitten's face. Being not so big myself, I felt a sort of kinship with this imaginary kitten. As if it were me. The other feature was no less heartwarming. This was a rectangular picture, about two inches by one inch, printed on the left side of the big box. It was the HMV emblem, which depicted a whiteandbrown beagle, Nipper, listening intently to music as a gramophone was being played. I experienced a deep familiarity with the dog, like the sort people develop with fictional characters or celebrities they watch daily on television. Both the imaginary kitten of the shiny, round stylus and the very real beagle listening to "his master's voice" evoked thoughtless affection from me. They were symbols of innocence, devotion, and love. Insofar as I felt such feelings toward my mother, these "animals" came to represent aspects of me. The fact that boundaries between reality and fantasy in a child's mind are tenuous facilitated my feeling one with these "animals" and, through them, with the gramophone itself.

A pause is indicated here. And, frankly, also a confession. The fantasies I have just alluded to were not known to me as a child. They are retrospective constructions of a middleaged psychoanalyst. Even the way I have described the gramophone is based solely upon my memory and imagination. The real thing, which I have not seen for nearly forty years, might look different. I don't know.

But let me move on with the story. A few years later, my mother died and I moved to my maternal grandfather's house in another city. I carried the gramophone with me and took excellent care of it. But when I was eighteen, just before I left for college, it needed repairs. I brought it to a trusted mechanic, who assured me that he would fix it and keep it safe for me until I returned on my break from school. When I did return, however, he was away at a wedding and his shop was closed. Then various commitments prevented me from returning. Time passed. I heard that the mechanic had died. A year or so later, I went to that town and located his house. I spoke to his son, who earnestly said that he would look into the matter. Yet the expression on his face left no doubt in my mind that the machine would never be found. I was right.

Paradoxically, the loss of the real gramophone gave birth to the gramophone in my imagination. I will always long for the actual gramophone, but I will never lose the gramophone as it exists in the inner world of my memory. The gramophone in the external reality is elusive. The one in my imagination is reliable. Like a good friend, it is always there, giving testimony to the secret power of physical objects in the realm of nostalgia.

Nostalgia

The more painful our separation from the things that have the most sentimental value, the more we cling to them in our reverie. We cannot—indeed, we refuse to—let them go. At the heart of nostalgia is the universal tendency to exalt what we have lost. We caress these lost objects with the soft flannel of longing, embellishing and idealizing them in the process. The pain of our loss feeds our love of the items. This sense of loss, and yet of gain, explains nostalgia's bittersweetness. It is bitter because it reminds us of our loss. It is sweet because it emanates from a mental reunion, as it were, with an idealized version of lost possessions and places.

However, traumatic loss is not the only source of nostalgia. In the course of our lives, we are inevitably separated from cherished physical possessions, like childhood toys and comic books. When lost, these objects are also exalted, and when unexpectedly "rediscovered," stir up memories that would otherwise remain buried in our minds.

Each generation has its own emotionally significant physical objects. Men and women who are now in their seventies are moved by the mention of wooden yo-yos, glass marbles, stove-top tin toasters, and the first Pyrex cooking pans that appeared on the market. The generation after them (the "baby boomers") waxes eloquently about jukeboxes, Handy Andy tool kits, and comic books. Even those in their thirties break into a wistful smile upon being reminded of the early video games like Pac-Man. Encounters with such "old things" stir up memories that would otherwise remain buried in our minds.

A senior colleague of mine, Allen Wheelis, eloquently captures the evocative quality of environmental cues that remind us of the past in his book *The Illusionless Man:*

> *We—all of us—go to cocktail parties, smile and talk and talk, we take care of children, and work, and take pride in what we do, and believe the trouble isn't there. But we fool ourselves. It's there, and we know it at night when the wind blows. And it's there, too, after analysis; for when you have been completely analyzed—whatever that may mean—when, at the end of the last hour of your, perhaps, third analysis, you shake hands with your analyst and leave his office for the last time—at just that moment you hear a song, a snatch of melody from the radio of a passing convertible, feel again the pressure of a girl's head on your shoulder when you danced with her to that song, years ago . . .*

the fumbling tenderness comes back and you feel an ache of longing . . . for something—not the girl, something else—something which has no name, lies beyond your grasp, and you know that analysis, however fine its net, could not capture this elusive anguish.

While it was not a tangible physical object but a piece of music that acted as a trigger for releasing the "fumbling tenderness" in this instance, the issue under consideration remains the same. Repudiated fragments of our past come back to us in all sorts of ways. The vault of amnesia enlists things in the external world as its messengers.

A red mailbox

In South Africa, where David Stein grew up, the postal service's mailboxes are red. When David emigrated to the United States as a young man, he was startled by this country's blue mailboxes. He still says that "blue mailboxes just don't do it for me." In other words, they do not provide him with a feeling of warmth, familiarity, and reassurance. His reaction to red mailboxes is entirely different. He gets excited just talking about them. When he sees them, during a business trip to London, or while vacationing in Bermuda, he feels a sudden rush of emotion. The red mailboxes speak to him with a sense of calm, strength, and resolve: "Yes, whatever you put inside us will reach its destination." They also evoke memories from his childhood and youth: mailing letters to a favorite uncle in Durban and, later, to his girlfriend, who had gone for a summer to England. The red mailboxes are special, he insists.

Like most immigrants, David is adept at transforming otherwise forgettable elements from his original home into unforgettable memories. Immigration involves separation from familiar people and places. Leaving friends and relatives hurts, but over time, the immigrant finds new neighbors, new friends and foes, new lovers, new drinking buddies, and a new life. Oftentimes the main trauma of immigration is not separation from people but separation from familiar landscapes and the physical objects that populate it. People are more or less the same everywhere. Places can differ so profoundly that an immigrant in a dramatically different place may no longer be able to have certain emotional experiences.

To compensate, the immigrant searches for places whose climate and vegetation match those of his original country. Indeed, he might become involved in a lifelong attempt at such symbolic restitution. Many immigrant friends of mine feel yearnings of this sort. Supriya Bhatia, who grew up in Kenya and now resides in Boston, feels a persistent desire to relocate to Southern California or New Mexico, which remind her of her childhood environment. Others, like Jean Brown, who came to this country from England, create a "back home" atmosphere in their current residences. Jean has made a beautiful English garden in her backyard. She even has planted irises and other bulbs that she brought from her mother's garden in suburban London. This assures her a sense of continuity across time and space.

The artist Giorgio de Chirico's preoccupation with Italian landscapes is a conspicuous example of such a need. Born of recently migrated parents in Greece, de Chirico grew up knowing dislocation and loneliness. His parents frequently moved from one home to another during his childhood, and his mother returned to Italy after her husband's death when de Chirico was eighteen years old. As an adult, he led a peripatetic life, frequently moving between Greece, Germany, Italy, and France, till he finally settled in Italy.

Throughout his life, de Chirico seemed to be searching for an environment that would be congenial and soothing, like a mother's body is to a child. Not surprisingly, his paintings are replete with allusions to travel and migration—horses, trains, and railroad stations—as well as the topographic nuances and architectural moods of his true motherland, Italy. Their titles tell a similar story: *The Departure of a Poet, The Anguish of Departure,* and *The Melancholy of Departure.* The last-mentioned painting is an especially powerful depiction of his desperate and lifelong homesickness.

Most immigrants are not so talented. To remember their homelands, they collect items like rugs, statues, wall hangings, decorative plates, bed covers—anything from the place they left behind. The immigrant's home becomes a refuge, these familiar objects offering solace in an unfamiliar land.

The exile has a much different relationship with things. Having had to leave against his will, escaping persecution, and being unable to enjoy the usual "protective rites of farewell," the exile regards his country of origin with profound ambivalence. His rage against the land that he was abruptly forced to leave makes him repudiate and deny positive experiences and attachments of the past, like a wronged husband who forgets the happy memories of his marriage. Moreover, the impossibility of returning to his homeland concentrates all his efforts in the direction of integration with the new surroundings. Nostalgia is alien to him and he has little use for physical objects of the past.

With the passage of time, however, the immigrant and the exile change places as far as their attitude about physical objects from "back home" is concerned. The immigrant becomes less passionate about such things. His aesthetic changes as a reflection of his feeling increasingly at home in his new country and as a consequence of the relationships he has developed there. He begins to draw more and more pleasure from the things of his adopted country. The exile, after many years, even decades, may start to reminisce about the customs, the landscape, and the physical objects of his original country. If he has succeeded and thrived in exile, he may be able to experience positive feelings toward his past, and therefore toward the objects that remind him of it.

Sometimes it falls to the next generation to reconnect with the "old country." My friend Sol Ackerman, whose father survived a Nazi concentration camp, recently bought a German cuckoo clock. This beautiful and efficient clock, acquired during a sabbatical in Heidelberg, represents Sol's (and, through him, his father's) belated acknowledgment of the good times his father had in Germany as a boy, long before the Holocaust. Sol never forgets to emphasize that the clock's design represents the pre-Hitler era of Germany. In this "nostalgia by proxy," the acquisition of a new object by a son celebrates the repudiated love of motherland by his father. The younger generation does what the older one was unable to do.

Remembering the dead

Perhaps no item has the power to evoke nostalgia more than one left behind by a loved one who has died. These legacies are heart-wrenching reminders of our loss, yet they play an important role in helping us establish a meaningful continuity between the dead and the living. They become bridges across the chasm of time and generations and ultimately serve life-enhancing purposes. Proust's description of his reaction to the death of his sweetheart, Albertine, testifies to the power physical objects have to create nostalgia in a time of mourning. He writes:

> *If all of a sudden I thought of her room, her room in which the bed stood empty, of her piano, her motorcar, I lost all my strength, I shut my eyes, let my head droop upon my shoulder like a person who is about to faint. . . . I stepped across the room with endless precautions, I took up a position from which I could not see Albertine's chair, the pianola upon the pedals of which she used to press her golden slippers, nor a single one of the things which she had used and all of which, in the secret*

language which my memory had imparted to them,
seemed to be seeking to give me a fresh translation,
a different version, to announce to me for a second
time the news of her departure.

After the initial disbelief and pain, the mourner is able to face the reality of her loss. Now the possessions of the deceased are divided into three categories: things that are thrown away, things that are given away, and things that are passed on as mementos and family heirlooms to the next generation. Most everyday items—toothbrushes, underwear, old household items—belong in the first category. The better-preserved garments and utensils figure in the second category. And precious china, jewelry, fine furniture, and objects of unique personal importance (e.g., journals, letters, a stamp collection, a handwritten manuscript) belong in the third category.

Sorting the deceased's possessions along these lines is an important step in the mourning process. Disposing of the everyday items can be the most difficult, as these are often the most intimate reminders of a person's existence. Emptying the closets and clearing out the medicine chest seems to erase them more completely than the reality of death. In grief, some may take years to remove these items. Others may hastily and immediately

dispose of a dead relative's physical possessions.
Both reactions suggest that the bereaved is having
difficulty facing the pain of loss. By quickly throw-
ing things away, she rapidly bypasses this pain and
doesn't allow it to simmer, as it should in normally
progressing grief. By keeping things for a long
time, she postpones pain. Both these manners of
handling things left by a dead person show an anguished reaction to loss. Both imply a difficulty in
coming to grips with the changed realities conse-
quent upon loss and the emotions stirred up by it.

In Judith Guest's *Ordinary People,* the saga of a
suburban family coming apart under the strain of
the accidental death of a teenage son, the room of
the dead boy is kept "frozen" in time. Months
pass, but nothing is changed, not one item moved
or disposed of. In Anne Tyler's *The Accidental
Tourist,* a description of the opposite phenome-
non appears. The book's protagonist, who has lost
his son in a freak shooting accident, throws away
all the latter's possessions. His wife chides him:

> *When Ethan died, you emptied his closet and his
> bureau as if you couldn't be rid of him soon enough.
> You kept offering people his junk in the basement,
> stilts and sleds and skateboards, and you couldn't
> understand why they didn't accept them. . . . There's
> something so muffled about the way you experience*

things, I mean love or grief or anything; it's like you are trying to slip through life unchanged.

The possessions in the third category—those items that will be passed down as keepsakes—connect us to our loved ones in two different ways: as ordinary mementos or as "linking objects." Mementos are owned proudly and used in a realistic way. Their connection with the deceased gradually becomes dim in the mind of the survivors. As a result, the survivors experience a comfortable sense of ownership of such objects. For instance, a young woman who receives her late grandmother's china may happily use it for serving dinner on festive occasions as a way to fondly remember her beloved relative.

While some items symbolize our love for the deceased, others become "linking objects," depositories of our intense love-hate attitude toward the deceased. These objects stir up searing emotional pain, dread, or fear. This pain and dread can be so severe that a "linking object" is kept hidden and removed from day-to-day contact. A peculiarly ambivalent attitude develops with regard to it. On the one hand, it cannot be seen or used due to the unpleasant feelings it evokes. On the other hand, it cannot be thrown away because doing so becomes tantamount to "murdering" its former owner. As a result, the object—say, a camera or a wristwatch—is kept safely but unused and out of sight. The survivor always knows its whereabouts even though she might ignore it for considerable lengths of time. The object exists as a frozen reservoir of feelings.

When mourning goes well, however, old objects help establish meaningful continuity between the dead and the living. They become bridges across the chasm of time and serve life-enhancing purposes. For instance, after his father's death, Vamik Volkan, a distinguished psychoanalyst, chose to keep his father's diary and his citizenship papers. Both items help nurture Vamik's identity as a Cypriot and his connection to his father. Stamped with his father's photograph, the citizenship papers resound with the turbulent history of his native island and of his family. Cherished and affirming, these documents, hanging on his wall, help nurture his identity and connection to his father.

Though their effect on us differs remarkably, the fact is that all such bequeathed objects exert an enormous amount of power over us. Sometimes this effect is laden with the anguish of loss and other times with the pride of legacy. Such objects are hardly emotion free. That much one can say with certainty.

Behind the scenes

Is the power attributed to old objects—especially those existing in the realm of fantasy—actual or merely embroidered out of the need for belonging and continuity? Daniel Geahchan tries to deconstruct the "nostalgic relationship" with old objects by suggesting that the nostalgic is not really looking for lost objects; he is looking for objects that have become retrospectively idealized. The pursuit is a mental one. And even that is a bit of sham since the nostalgic's real longing is for a retrospectively manufactured state of self-innocence. That state never existed in reality. It is all a mirage.

If Geahchan is correct, then the reasons for our liking Norman Rockwell's paintings begin to shift a bit. We think that we like these works because they remind us of the "good old times" when people were nicer, time moved slowly, and life was easy. But now it appears that we have allowed ourselves to be tricked. Look at one such painting and ask yourself the following questions: Would you really enjoy spending an hour in that barbershop? What would you and the barber talk about? What if the dog sleeping near his feet was not as friendly as it seems in the painting? And how do we know that the boy getting a haircut is not a real brat?

Now, what about Grandmother's china? Or Dad's watch? Those red mailboxes or even my mother's gramophone? Do they harken back to an actuality or a mirage? Most likely, a bit of both. Nostalgic things are deceptive in their emotional appeal. We do not get as fulfilled as we thought we might when presented, in reality, with lost objects from our past. The relief provided by nostalgic objects turns out to be momentary. Nostalgia keeps us spellbound but, in the end, leaves us tied to our naive illusions.

The allure of such magic, however, is great. It has led to an entire culture of relics and reminis-cences. Norman Rockwell is but one icon of the tradition that ranges from the morose ruminations of that great nostalgic of France, Marcel Proust, to the sly entrepreneurial instinct of that curious New Englander Wallace Nutting.

Who was Wallace Nutting?

A highly private man who published a detailed auto-biography and a lover of the past who used the most modern media available to him to celebrate that past, Wallace Nutting (1861–1941) made an indel-ible mark on the early-twentieth-century American culture. A Congregational minister in Connecticut, Nutting left the pulpit at the age of forty-three to lecture and write about his romanticized vision of American history. Soon he assembled a large collection of reproduction furniture and wrought-iron decorative accessories that he used as props for taking photographs of ordinary folks dressed up in Colonial costumes. These forged scenes were intended to evoke respect and longing for the "idyllic times" of America's past.

A celebrity preacher turned salesman of nostalgia, Nutting was strikingly prolific and successful. He produced more than five million photographs of pastoral landscapes and quaint interiors. They were hand-colored, at first by himself and then by the large coterie of workers at his rural Connecticut factory. By the 1920s, there was hardly a middle-class home, at least on the East Coast, that was without a Nutting photograph.

Relentless in his idealization of the past, Nutting could hardly remain satisfied by taking staged photographs. He sold his props and the house that had served as his studio and moved on to manufacturing and selling period furniture. Still later, he produced a series of books referred to as the *States Beautiful* books, which include narratives and anecdotes about various American states as well as numerous hand-tinted photographs he took during his travels around the country.

What is fascinating about Wallace Nutting is

that he was simultaneously an artist and an impostor (remember, his photographs were all staged), loner and showman, and dreamer and merchant. Above all, he was a master at exploiting the ordinary human vulnerability to overvalue what is lost and to idealize the customs of a bygone era. Take one look at his interiors and you will recognize what I am talking about. Besides the "old" furniture, you will note what the women in these photographs are doing. Just as actual women of that time were acquiring voting rights, seeking education, and entering the work force, Nutting offered society at large pictures of women cooking, sewing, playing the piano, and, in essence, staying within the confines of the home. In these depictions, the present is rejected while the past is idealized and made desirable. This is the same trick that Norman Rockwell plays; the same trick mementos play on us if we are not careful.

Putting old things to new use

Photo albums, family heirlooms, and even those things we can no longer retrieve from the black holes of passing time play a significant psychological role in our lives by helping us connect with our personal and cultural history. But inordinate sentimentality about them is an impediment to an emotionally rich life in the "here and now." Ideal⸱ization creates mirages, not destinations.

The red mailbox, for instance, is a means for my South African friend to think about the neighbor⸱hood where he first saw it and the letters he wrote during his years in Johannesburg. Who were the in⸱tended recipients of those missives? What was his relationship to them? What was he communicating to them and how did he want them to respond? Above all, where are those people now to whom he wrote all those letters? What happened to his rela⸱tionships with them and why? Nostalgic objects are more useful as triggers for deepening self⸱knowledge than as actual things in themselves. This way they can perform the important psycho⸱logical function of linking us with unknown aspects of our past and also with deeper facets of our loved ones with whom that past was constructed and spent. "Old things" are good not because they are inherently wonderful but because they are psycho⸱logically enhancing and useful.

Back to the gramophone

It was big, brown, and warm to touch.

Thinking about it, reflecting upon its potential meanings for her and for me, has contributed to my knowing more about the first two decades of my life. I can feel the emotional texture of those years more fully, can assimilate them into my current life. So, yes, the gramophone—as it exists in my memory—is of considerable psychological benefit to me. It makes me think of my mother and our good times together. It gives me strength. This is how it should be.

But once in a while some dreadful questions crop up in my mind. Could I have inadvertently played a role in the gramophone's misplacement? Was my taking it in for repairs right before leaving town unconsciously intended to get rid of the machine? Was I getting tired of taking care of it for a decade following my mother's death? It is painful and embarrassing to entertain these questions, but it is necessary to face them. The gramophone was not only an affectionate link to my mother but also a constant and painful reminder of her absence. In "misplacing" it, might I have hoped to misplace that grief as well?

I feel that I can finally let go of the pursuit of the gramophone in reality. Even the gramophone in my imagination appears less desirable. Yet something tugs at me. What to do? Look for the actual gramophone all over again? I resist the desire but at times weaken in my resolve. Mesmerized by the innocent relentlessness of this desire, I melt. Give in.

Maybe this time when I go to India . . .

sacred things

The lecture hall is full.

Nearly three hundred people are listening to me talk about the hazards of reckless optimism. I can see that they are intrigued by my suggestion that a taste of hopelessness is as essential in life as the experience of hope. Lack of hope destroys the capacity to go on despite hardships. Lack of hopelessness makes one cling to unrealistic dreams. The audience is engaged, and I, like a tightrope walker, am raptly absorbed in what I am doing. One step at a time.

And then suddenly everything falls apart.

I notice that a young man in the front row is sitting with his feet resting on a stack of books. The sight makes me sick. I lose my train of thought and can no longer go on smoothly with the lecture. Seeing someone put his feet—shoes and all—on top of books disturbs me greatly. I keep talking but am now divided within myself. One part of me says, "Ignore him. Go on with what you are talking about." Another part is indig‹ nant. It protests, asking me to say to this guy, "Don't you know that books are sacred?"

But are they? Being the son of parents who were writers and the grandson of a devoutly religious man who extolled the *Ahl-e-Kitaab* (the People of the Book), I grew up regarding books as sacred. In fact, any paper with printed words—flyers, news‹ papers, letters—was regarded as sacrosanct in our home. Placing it on the floor and putting feet on it was deemed utterly rude, if not "sinful." Such an upbringing led me to develop a lifelong reverence for books. I feel they are sacred. But others might question my use of the word *sacred* in this context. Therefore let us begin by explicitly defining our terms here.

What do we mean by *sacred*?

The dictionary definition of the word *sacred* reads "dedicated or set up for the service or worship of a deity." It seems pretty straightforward. Our emo‹ tional experience of sacred things is, however, far more complex. And this necessitates a closer scrutiny of the feelings that come together to form the gestalt of sacredness. There are four such components.

REVERENCE. A sacred object is first and foremost an exalted object. We place it on a higher level than our own selves. We feel that it belongs on an entirely different plane. In contrast to our humdrum and mundane existence, the sacred object has a sublime and transcendental quality about it. We feel humble when we encounter such an object. We imbue it with higher authority and endow it with transformative potential. We emotionally prostrate ourselves in front of it and bask in its mesmerizing effect upon us.

CIRCUMSCRIPTION. A second attribute of sacred things is that there are strict limits and boundaries for their use and for our contact with them. All sorts of rules and rituals are associated with their place and function in our lives. Indeed, the Hebrew word for *sacred* or *holy* is *qadosh,* which is derived from the verb *qadish,* or "to set apart." A sacred object is therefore something that is set apart from the plebian things surrounding it. This is not merely metaphorical. Churches, synagogues, mosques, and temples are testimony to the public efforts we make toward the spatial accommodation of sacred objects. Even within homes, special

77

places are created for sacred objects, and non-sacred things are not allowed to be kept there. Moreover, the "sacred" things cannot be mixed with things that are deemed "profane."

The anguished response of the North American Hindu community to the depiction of their elephant-headed deity, Ganesha, on a toilet seat by a Seattle-based bathroom fixture manufacturer proves this point. More familiar is the uproar created by New York Catholics in response to the Brooklyn Museum of Art displaying an exhibit called "Piss Christ," which literally consisted of a crucifix in a jar filled with urine. Even in less drastic settings, it is hardly conceivable to put sacred objects in a place not "suitable" for them. Imagine a holy cross or a mezuzah on the entry door to a strip club and you will immediately know what I am talking about. The symbolic representatives of sacred objects also require proper placement. An inscription saying *Allah-o-Akbar* ("God is Great") in Arabic appearing on a bottle of whiskey and a Star of David imprinted on a package of pork sausages are bound to create an uproar among the believers of the respective faiths these emblems represent.

DIVINITY. Sacred objects are customarily linked with belief in God. Whether the non-believers among us have objects that they regard as "sacred" is something I will address shortly. From dictionary definitions to the practices of billions of people all over the globe, the word *sacred* re‹ mains intricately linked with religion. To be sure, national flags and political emblems are capable of evoking no less strong sentiments. Nonetheless, the reverence and circumscription that is associated with sacred objects is most marked in the realm of religion. Ask a Christian entering St. Peter's Basil‹ ica, a Jew standing next to the Wailing Wall, and a Muslim looking at the *Kaa'ba Sharif* during his pilgrimage to Mecca, and you will note the degree to which these brick‹and‹mortar structures are linked with the idea of God in their minds.

FAITH. The fourth and final emotional compo‹ nent of regarding something as sacred is faith. This implies a deep trust in the veracity of the object's claim to be exempt from the ordinary rules of logic. A devout Hindu, for instance, would not question the existence of *Hanuman,* the widely worshipped monkey god from the epic *Ramayana,* nor would a believing Muslim raise an eyebrow upon the mention of *Burraq,* the winged horse that transported Mohammed overnight from Mecca to Jerusalem. An earnest Catholic takes the Immacu‹ late Conception as a matter of fact, just as an Or‹ thodox Jew regards a piece of Middle Eastern land as actually having been assigned to him by God.

These are tenaciously held beliefs. They are beyond logical inquiry. Such surrender of skepticism is a necessary precondition for worship.

Idol worship

At a superficial glance, the matter of idol worship appears clear. Judeo-Christian and Islamic traditions forbid idolatry, while the pre-Judaic pagans, Mayans, Hindus, and other scattered "primitive" people of today allow or even extol it. A deeper look, however, challenges such simplistic thinking. The fact is that followers of all religions employ exalted and revered inanimate objects in the course of worship. Catholics are especially accused of idolatry because they frequently adorn their churches with images of saints. The reverence associated with taking the wafer of Communion or the unrolling of the Torah during a Bar Mitzvah also speaks to the pervasive role of sacred objects in Judeo-Christian religious practices. Less dramatic evidence of the same sort is provided by how a believing Christian treats a holy cross and an observant Jew a menorah. Muslims have their crescent and Hindus a vast panoply of icons and emblems. Fascinatingly, Muslims who deride Hindus for idolatry themselves perform a variety of stone‑kissing and pebble‑throwing rituals during their pilgrimage to Mecca.

The fact is that such matters are far from simple. On the one hand, there are practices that ap‑ pear suspiciously akin to "idol worship" in Judeo‑ Christian and Islamic traditions. On the other hand, most thoughtful Hindus acknowledge that their idols are merely way stations to a supreme God that is formless and beyond reification. Indeed, there are many Hindus *(nirankaaris)* who worship God without the aid of any material icons at all.

By and large, though, the deployment of mate‑ rial emblems and statues in the course of worship is pervasive. It is found in all religions, though the usual tendency is to regard the peripheral aspects of others' religion as central points of their belief and practice. A bigger problem, I think, has re‑ sulted from taking the word *idol* in this context too literally. Thus one who has statues and pic‑ tures in his place of worship is called "idolater," and the one who does not is absolved from such "accusation." This is a superficial form of thinking. To my mind, idol worship occurs when the deity worshipped is not transcendent and divine at all but ephemeral and banal. Instead of mobilizing one toward a sense of unity with the world, such "worship" remains focused upon narrow personal interests. Take the example of someone who adores money and puts financial acquisition above everything else. From his vantage point, a rich man is a good man and a poor man a bad man, regardless of all other attributes that each might or might not possess. This is idol worship in my definition, for it has replaced transcendence by narcissism. The self has taken the place of God; it has become an idol. The same is true of people who are fame worshippers, power worshippers, and so on. Idol worship, it turns out, has less to do with inanimate objects and more with corruption of our value systems. But this is not all. Our foray through the cloister of sacred objects reveals still other mysteries in this realm. The biggest among them is the distinction between what is "sacred" and what is "profane."

Sacred versus profane

An important question that pertains to the concept of sacred objects is this: If everything has been created by God, shouldn't everything be sacred? And, as a corollary, one might ask, If everything is sacred, then what is the point in calling something—or anything, for that matter— sacred? The trouble does not stop here. For considerations of the sort I have just raised compel us to ask, If everything is sacred, then aren't we saying that nothing is profane? What, then, is the conceptual or practical use of the "sacred" concept? After all, there is no sound without silence and no light without darkness. There is no wetness without dryness and no death without life. A dichotomy depends upon the existence of two poles. Therefore, we cannot call something "sacred" without labeling (at least implicitly) other things as either "non-sacred," "banal," or even "profane."

This line of thinking finds support from the etymological roots of *sacred* and *profane*. The former is derived from the Latin words *sacren,* meaning "to consecrate," and *sacrare,* meaning "akin to." *Sacred* therefore means something that connects us to the universe and helps us transcend our self-oriented existence. It has a spiritual and religious connotation. The word *profane,* in contrast, is derived from the Latin *profanus,* itself comprised of *pro,* or "before," and *fanum,* or "temple." In other words, *profane* means something that has been left outside of the temple. A line of sanctity seems to have been drawn here and a boundary created. Sacred is in and profane is out.

While clarifying on one count, this view leaves something to be desired on another. It positions sacred things as links to the divine and profane things as not possessing that power. However, it does not explain the riddle that if God created everything, then how come some things ended up being profane?

Further complexity arises if one takes the perspective of the non-believer. For her, God does not exist. The creation of the universe and the evolution of man are to be explained by scientific methods alone. One can certainly have awe for the mysteries in these realms, but there is hardly any need for regarding anything as sacred or profane. Things are what they are. Simply because someone imbues an object with spiritual mumbo jumbo does not render it any closer to God, who does not exist anyway. Moreover, the fact that sacred objects of one group are not deemed so by others confirms that sacred objects are man-made instruments for personal solace and group cohesion. They serve emotional, social, and political purposes. They are not God-given. Sanctity is not inherent to their nature.

As we can see, the believer and the non-believer address the sacred versus profane dichotomy in diametrically opposite ways. For the believer, some things are sacred because they are material bridges to a transcendental union with the supreme God. For the non-believer, the division is the product of a spurious idea to begin with, namely that God exists. The two positions are difficult to reconcile in their literal extremes. However, if one takes into account that the non-believer might also have things that she looks up to and respects deeply, the possibility of bringing the two sides together emerges. Take, for instance, my friend David Long, a psychoanalyst who owns a handwritten letter of Sigmund Freud from some eighty years ago. He keeps it with utmost care and feels great pride in owning it. He experiences respect, humility, and near-awe every time he takes it out to show someone. So would we be correct in saying that the letter is a "sacred" thing for him? One could argue that it is, but then someone else would say that this is an improper use of the word. In the end, therefore, it seems to be a matter of semantics and convention, and there the spiritual-religious connotation of the word *sacred* wins the day.

Sacredness and history

Our psychoanalyst friend's love affair with a handwritten document by Freud demonstrates the link highly cherished things often have with history. The question is whether the same is true of sacred things. And the answer seems to be in the affirmative. The factual or mythic linkage of a physical object to places and personages of dee p religious significance plays a large role in making it "sacred."

The reverence displayed by Christians toward the Shroud of Turin, which ostensibly covered the face of Jesus Christ after his death, is an example of this. Another example is the profound respect Muslims have for *Moo-e-Mubarak,* or hairs that purportedly came from Mohammad's scalp or beard. Families descended from highly placed Islamic clerics in the Middle East claim to have them, and a single hair is preserved at the mosque in Hazrat bal, a little town in Kashmir, India. That country happens to be the *font origio* of Hinduism and has numerous sites containing relics associated with revered Hindu saints and *avatars* (reincarnated embodiments of a particular god). Towns like Mathura and Ayodhya are, for instance, regarded as the birthplaces of Krishna and Rama, respectively, and are therefore felt to be holy places.

Lest all this appear peculiar, one simply needs to be reminded of the Old City of Jerusalem. Within an area of one square kilometer are some of the holiest shrines of the Judaic, Christian, and Islamic faiths. Most prominent include the Jewish holy sites of the Western Wall and the old synagogues of Elijah the Prophet and Yohanan ben Zakai; the Christian holy sites of the Via Dolorosa (the street on which Jesus is believed to have traveled from his trial to his Crucifixion), the Church of the Holy Sepulcher, and the Church of Saint

Anne; and the Muslim holy sites of the *Haram-al-Sharif* ("Temple Mount"), the Dome of the Rock, and Al-Aqsa Mosque. All in all, the Old City is replete with the history of three of the world's great religions. It is this historical linkage that gives the place its sanctity and sacredness. Knowing this, a cynic might ask whether Jerusalem was sacred before the rise of Judaism, Christianity, and Islam. And if not, does the "pre-sacred" core of the city continue to exist on some geological or conceptual plane? The fact is that "sacred," "non-sacred," or, in this instance, "pre-sacred" are all human constructions. There is nothing inherent in a given area of land or, for that matter, in a particular physical object that makes it sacred. It is we who, for our emotional needs, ascribe such qualities to them. As a result, those who need such markers take them concretely. They are offended by the questioning of the veracity of their views. Others who are less emotionally needy of "sacred" things fearlessly entertain questions of the sort mentioned above. They can even put such quandaries to creative and playful use. Salman Rushdie's controversial book *Satanic Verses*, which created an uproar in the Islamic world, is a case in point here.

Sacredness and beauty

The relationship between sacredness and beauty is a complicated one. To begin with, it is hard to define beauty. In general, though, we call something beautiful when it provides us visual pleasure, and this, in turn, results from a certain kind of balance and synthesis. A beautiful thing (e.g., a majestic grandfather clock, an intricately woven rug, a gorgeously appointed automobile, a sharp-looking digital camera) offers us an optimal mixture of soothing and exciting sensations. It pleases our eyes by subtly evoking the innocent wonder of childhood, and it stirs our imagination by stimulating our inner fantasy world. We are satisfied and left wanting at the same time. And we love the feeling.

But what does all this have to do with sacred things? Well, there seems to be a prevalent sense that sacred things are inherently beautiful. Mostly this is true. But why? Perhaps the awe they inspire in us colors our visual perception of them. Or perhaps, since we assign beauty to God, a sacred thing that is a pathway to Him automatically becomes beautiful in our eyes. Moreover, if we believe that everything is God's creation, then each and every physical object—a razor blade, a shirt, a desk, a mailbox, an elevator—begins to appear complete and harmonious in itself. The entire world becomes an object of beauty. Even what might be regarded conventionally as ugly can appear unconventionally beautiful given such a perspective.

This sort of conceptual traffic moves in both directions. In other words, not only do sacred things appear inherently beautiful, beautiful things can appear inherently sacred. After all, the achievement of beauty gives testimony to man's or nature's success in creating a certain sort of organic harmony. This can be interpreted, by the believers, as an indication of the sort of oneness with God that lies at the root of a sacred experience. The colloquialism about a well-dressed woman looking "divine" captures the essence of what I am trying to say here.

Beauty and sacredness also encounter each other in the places of worship. From overdone splendor to soft-spoken elegance, consideration of aesthetics inevitably gets woven in the fabric of man's prayer. Churches, synagogues, mosques, and temples are often the most beautiful architectural sites in a nation. From Michelangelo's painting on the Sistine Chapel's ceiling to the sensual sculptures of India's Khajuraho, and from the lavishly appointed Buddhist temples in the Far East to the breathtaking, intricate Islamic prayer rugs from Iran, aesthetic achievement and veneration of religious deities go hand in hand.

What does this tell us? Does this beautification constitute homage to the Almighty, or does it betray anxiety about the strength of one's convictions? Would one respect God any less if he "resided" in less opulent quarters? Or is the ornateness of a religious place a sort of public relations maneuver? "Make the place irresistible and they will come." It is also possible that the beauty of such places is intended to induce peacefulness in those in attendance. "Look, life is not all bad," it seems to say. And once you have been put in a cheerful and optimistic mood, you are more open to hearing the preacher's message. Or as the non-believer would say, you are ready to be hypnotized and brainwashed. If this explanation of why places of worship are well-decorated is plausible, it is not a reassuring commentary upon the inherent power of religion.

In all fairness, though, I must acknowledge the existence of ascetic orders in all major religious faiths. Followers of these sects shun fanfare and ostentatiousness. They lead simple lives, and their places of worship, if they even construct such institutions, are devoid of the dollop of extraneous beauty that is often added to the cup of faith. Is such disengagement of man-made beauty and sacredness more respectful of God? Or is it a repudiation of his having given us the capacity to make beautiful things? What is going on here?

My original quandary:
Are books sacred?

Remember my emotional outrage at the young man who was sitting in the lecture hall with his feet on top of a stack of books? Now, as we are coming to the conclusion of our discourse on sacred things, you might ask whether I told him to remove his feet from the books. Well, the fact is I did. There was simply no other way for me to continue with my lecture peacefully. Books are sacred for me and, if you'll pardon the expression, his treating them with a lack of reverence bothered the hell out of me.

However, over the years that have passed since this incident, I have given the matter some more thought. I now wonder if I was being too literal in my view of what is or is not sacred. While I still feel uneasy if someone steps on a newspaper or a magazine, I do not cringe as badly as before. This change is perhaps a result of many factors, continued self-reflection and growing older the most prominent among them. Having come across a huge number of worthless books has also helped, though I am sure you know that I say this in a tongue-in-cheek fashion. More seriously, I was nudged in the direction of softening my stance by a younger friend of mine named Kimberly Best. Kim is devoutly religious and yet she made me see that while my values might be admirable, their rigidity is not. She once gave me a Bible with the following inscription:

> *Let all of your other books be sacred objects, but not this one. I have chosen a nice, sturdy Bible for you. This book is made to stand on, both literally and figuratively. Write in it, toss it on the floor of your car, buy a new one when this gets old. The information in the book is sacred, the book is not!*

sexy things

Imagine you are a seventeen-year-old boy.

You are in eleventh grade and have a weekly art class that you are required to take. Your art teacher is Mrs. Tenner, Edye Tenner. She is in her early forties and has a beautiful face with luscious lips and deep, dark brown eyes. The little diamond studs in her ears sparkle each time she straightens her hair. She wears a skirt and a blouse. The cut of the blouse's neck reveals the beginning of her milky shoulders. An elegant string of pearls adorns her neck. Her breasts are full and round. They move gracefully as she breathes. At times you can see the vague outline of her nipples under her blouse. Well-coiffed yet shower fresh, she always smells good.

When she comes and stands next to you to look at the project you are working on, your heart starts to pound. Your mouth becomes dry and your body catches fire. You begin having visions of her naked body. You want to pounce on her, grab her, rip her clothes off her body, and make love to her. No, no, no. Making love is not what you have in mind. You want to fuck her. Fuck her hard. And hard is what you have become. Like the baseball bat in your locker. The only thing harder is to keep your erection hidden from her and your urges under control. The knowledge that you will soon jerk off in the school bathroom helps you remain somewhat calm.

What is going on here?

Is what I have just described merely the result of sexual hormones raging in the blood of a healthy teenager? Does erotic desire of this kind emanate solely from gonads and obscure command centers in the hypothalamic area of the brain? Or do we need a psychological explanation as well? After all, what we have here is a young boy on the verge of manhood, a beautiful "older" woman, her unseen but nonetheless ever-present husband (remember, she is *Mrs.* Tenner), and sexual desire across socially constructed boundaries. The ground is thus ripe for the good old Oedipus complex to start acting up again. In other words, what Freud had described in the context of early childhood (namely, a boy's desire for his mother, renounced out of fear and love of the father) has remobilized during adolescence, except characters from outside the family have been enlisted to play the key roles. Like the hormonal explanation preceding it, this one seems apt but somehow incomplete.

Both vantage points leave the canvas of possibility less than optimally explored. To begin with, they take my introducing the topic of sexy things with the example of a boy (and not a girl) for granted. And they overlook the emphasis upon visual pathways to erotic stimulation. The boy's excitement seems to result from what is visible to him. There is no mention of whether Mrs. Tenner is an intelligent, kind, and generous person. Her attractiveness is described almost solely in terms of how she looks and what she wears. Skirt, blouse, diamonds, and pearls appear prominently here. What does such fascination with surface and indifference to depth tell us about the things men find sexy? And the next logical question is whether what is found sexy by men is also found sexy by women, or do sexy things for men and women differ from each other?

What turns men on?

When it comes to feeling sexual excitement, men are largely "visual beasts." Study after study has confirmed that physical beauty is what men seek most when looking for a sexual or romantic partner. They value looks more than women do, and this holds true all over the world. Indeed, in a 1990 study conducted in thirtyseven different cultures, no culture was found in which women cared more about the looks of their partners than men did.

Men's fascination with women's good looks is evident everywhere. Take personal ads, for example. While few descriptions in "Women Seeking Men" include comments upon men's physical attributes, they almost always contain references to women's own beauty. Words like "leggy," "slim," and "beautiful" and even "sensuous," "sultry," and "voluptuous" frequently appear in these ads. An informal survey of personal ads in an ethnic newspaper revealed that comments about one's physical attractiveness were included by 33 percent of men and 68 percent of women. This seems an accommodation to the "market's demands." Women are simply stating what men want to hear. Without the promise of a visual feast, they would not proceed to the table, so to speak.

Men also decide quickly and largely based upon looks whether or not they "like" a woman and would want a second date with her. They are notorious for talking about women's appearances, ranking each on a numerical scale (remember Bo Derek, a resounding 10!), and even taking pride in being a "leg man" or a "breast man," depending upon their fancying this or that body part of women.

Pornography is another realm in which men's visual propensity is evident. Almost ten million American adults read *Playboy* every month, and the magazine's total paid U.S. circulation is larger than *Esquire, GQ* and *Rolling Stone* combined. Regional editions of *Playboy* are published in seventeen countries: Brazil, Bulgaria, Croatia, the Czech Republic, France, Germany, Greece, Hungary, Italy, Japan, the Netherlands, Romania, Russia, Slovakia, Slovenia, Spain, and Taiwan. And, to be sure, the publishing and video world of pornography is not restricted to the *Playboy* enterprise. There are many such magazines and numerous "adult stores" throughout the nation. All in all, pornography is an $8-billion-a-year industry, and according to the *Report of the U.S. Commission on Obscenity and Pornography,* the patrons of adult bookstores and X-rated movie theaters are "predominately white middle-class, middle-aged, married men."

The pornographic image not only stirs up sexual excitement but also provides an avenue for the discharge of hostility. Even in the absence of bondage, submission, and overt forms of sadomasochism, the one whose naked body is on display is not someone who inspires feelings of tenderness and affection. The emotions mobilized by pornography, putting aside moralistic attitudes, boil down to basic animal lust. Such "lust" contains a hefty dose of contempt and hostility. Robert Stoller, who investigated the psychology of pornography in detail, concluded that in this enterprise "there is always a victim, no matter how disguised: no victim, no pornography." The human object of a pornographic gaze is invariably a debased one. This remains true despite the strip joint acquiring the dignified label "gentlemen's club" and regardless of whether we are talking of seedy bars in New Jersey, adult entertainment houses in South Carolina, or plush taverns in Tokyo, Bangkok, and New Orleans. However culturally sanctified and aesthetically adorned such places might be, their dancers remain nothing but quivering pieces of flesh. The emotional life of these women is of no consequence to the viewer, who has reduced them to mere things. Linda Lovelace, the star of the 1970s pornographic blockbuster *Deep Throat*, for instance, would be an unlikely college commencement speaker. She and others like her are not people one listens to; they are merely to be looked at. If this is not hostile debasement, what is?

But what precisely is it that men are looking for or, should we say, looking at? Certainly not the "real thing." Female genitalia does not constitute the focus of their gaze. Hardcore porn is less titillating than the excitement caused by the erotic hints and promises of soft porn. Most men are actually a little nervous about casting a studied glance at the female genital proper. Freud declared that "we never regard the genitals themselves, which produce the strongest sexual excitation, as really beautiful." Ariel Arango, a psychoanalyst practicing in Argentina, elaborates this finding in words that are pithy and succinct:

> *As a matter of fact, if we conducted a random survey among men, asking them for an accurate description of the vulva—its shape, size, and color—we would have a puzzling result: they are not able to do so. . . . Only then would they notice with surprise that they hardly look at it when making love. They hardly ever stop to observe the details of the "secret entrance." Even those who enjoy* lambendo lingua genitalia *(licking the genitals) would realize that they do not study it thoroughly. A man who has no difficulty in recalling the smallest features of a drawing, or the slightest lines of a statue, or the most delicate typographies of a book, will not be able, however, to describe the vulva accurately! It would be difficult to find a territory so much ignored by men as the geography of the* cunt.

The fact is that the visual "turn-on" that men so desperately depend upon comes from body parts that are *away* from the genitals: eyes, neck, shoulders, breasts, waist, legs, feet, and toes. And it is the adornment, enhancement, and highlighting of these "non-genital" parts of a woman's body by clothes, shoes, belts, fragrances, and all sorts of cosmetic accoutrements that result in men's sexual excitement. Victoria's Secret, while offering women rightful pride and pleasure in their bodies, is actually a men's store par excellence.

Sexy things, for men, are items that draw attention away from the genitals of a woman: lipstick, bras and panties, fishnet stockings, high-heeled shoes, necklaces, and dangling earrings. This paraphernalia does offer certain visual, tactile, and olfactory gratifications, but it functions primarily as an anaesthetic against the imagined dangers of actual physical sexuality. What Freud had said about the nature of fetishism (namely, that the fetishist requires an additional item on the body of a woman for feeling sexually aroused) turns out to be ubiquitous in male erotic excitement. Men boast of being straightforward in the matters of sexuality. The fact, however, is that they need distractions to reach their goal.

Such psychological explanations do not exhaust

the reasons why the reddening of the lips by lipstick, the narrowing of the waistline by a belt, the exaggeration of height by high-heeled shoes, and the youthfulness caused by Botox injections and silicone implants turn men on. In fact, as we look further, we find that factors far deeper than male anxiety about female genitals contribute to men's visual appetite for the accoutrements of female beauty. But first, let's consider the things women find sexy.

Things women find sexy

Did you know that:

- The annual circulation of *Playgirl* is nine times less than that of *Playboy,* and there are far fewer female customers of pornography in general.

- The market for pictures of naked males largely caters to homosexual men and not to heterosexual women.

- The women's magazine *Viva* began with offering nude male centerfolds à la *Playboy* but soon discontinued it. Its readers did not seem terribly interested in such material.

- Unlike the notorious "Peeping Tom," there is no entity called "Peeping Maria." Voyeurism, as a clinical syndrome, does not exist in women.

- Women make a choice of mate far more slowly than men do. Not that they do not take physical attractiveness of their potential partner into account, but they give it less weight than the qualities of sincerity, reliability, and monetary stability.

- Male fashion models make much less money than their female counterparts. This is the opposite of the ordinary pattern of incomes whereby in all professions men make more money than women.

These observations tell us that women are far less dependent upon visual cues for romantic and sexual arousal. Indeed, a recent worldwide study failed to find a single culture in which women rate "looks" as a more important mate selection variable than men do. Women are simply not that way. Their excitement comes from emotional gratification and not visual titillation. Women are more likely to be turned on by romance novels that portray rich and powerful men overcoming all sorts of difficulties for the sake of everlasting love than by porn.

This is not to say that women are not interested in beauty. They are. But their interest is largely in their own beauty and not so much in that of men. They lay out resources and spend money on self-enhancement and not on watching men's bodies. They buy cosmetics, perfumes, jewelry, handbags, belts, shoes, and figure-enhancing clothes to appear attractive to men; they know that this is what gets men's attention. And it is for the same reason that they take note of other women's beauty and its highlighting by makeup, attire, and ornaments. The idea is to quietly observe the competitor and learn the "tricks of the trade" from her.

The fascinating consequence of this is that sexy things for men are found in women's closets, and that's exactly where the sexy things for women are found. Men's suitcases turn out to be empty when it comes to sexy objects. This is not to say that women do not like their men to be well groomed and might not have preferences for this or that body type or item of clothing. They do. My friend Susan Kulovsky, who is a public relations attorney in Los Angeles, confided in me that men in black polo shirts make her tingle. And Sheela Sonalkar, a news broadcaster from Chicago, told me that she gets terribly turned on by men smoking pipes. However, one or two examples of such sort pale in comparison to the magnitude of "things" that turn men on.

Even the physical attributes of men that excite women seem less related to attractiveness per se and more to their implicit link to the man's social and financial status. A study by the social anthropologist John Marshall Townsend showed people pictures of men and women who ranged aesthetically

from "very good looking" to "unattractive" and pro-
fessionally from having high- to low-paying jobs.
The subjects were asked whom they would like to
go out with, have sex with, and even marry. While
men consistently preferred beautiful women regardless of their socioeconomic status, women rated
high-status but less attractive men as more desirable than more attractive men with lesser monetary
resources. At its simplest, men look for beauty and
women look for status.

But what does this mean? Are a boy's idealization of his mother and a girl's seeking protection
from her father sufficient to explain this difference? Not really. Such factors might play a role,
but deeper determinants seem to be at work (after
all, a boy also idealizes his father and a girl her
mother).

Enter, Charles Darwin

The rapidly developing field of "evolutionary aesthetics" comes to our rescue here. Elaborating upon
the ideas proposed by Charles Darwin (1809–1882)
in his classic book *The Origin of Species,* this recent
discipline explains our preferences in the realm of
beauty and physical attractiveness by tracing their
roots to the evolutionary history of mankind. In
other words, it suggests that what we find sensually

appealing is only so because it serves evolution— ary purposes and assures the propagation of our species. Beauty is merely a billboard for reproduc- tive health. Such a view takes out some personal drama from erotic emotions, but that should not preclude our serious consideration of it.

To keep the account sheets balanced, let us be- gin this time with women and their aesthetic pref- erences. We have already noted that women are less dependent upon visual cues for erotic stimula- tion. Being "less dependent" upon visual cues, however, does not mean that they are not at all turned on by what they see in men who might be potential romantic partners. So let us ask, What is it that they like in men, and how do such prefer- ences link to deeper, evolutionary imperatives?

Nancy Etcoff, the author of *Survival of the Pretti- est*, has extensively reviewed the writings of evolu- tionary aesthetics. According to her, women are turned on by evidences of dominance and status in men. They find men with above-average height, V-shaped torsos, strong arms, and erect posture at- tractive. Facial structure that is oval or rectangular with heavy brow ridges, deep-set eyes, a muscular jaw, and a prominent chin is also endearing to women. These features are experienced by them as signs of dominance and strength. This, in turn, provides unspoken clues to the man's ability to be protective toward a woman and her future children. According to the evolutionary scientists of beauty, like Richard Dawkins, this is the ultimate female turn-on. Whether a woman actually wants to have a child with the man is immaterial. These cues have served our female ancestors well for millennia and have thus become "hardwired" in the female brain. The possibility of having a protective mate who will be a reliable partner in raising children has become deeply ingrained in the female of our species and drives the pattern of its visual scanning.

But what does all this have to do with sexy things?

Any and all material accoutrements that highlight the male physical robustness and social power end up becoming "sexy things" for women. A tall man wearing an Irish tweed jacket with elbow patches and having a full head of thick hair appears more attractive to women than one who is stooped, bald, and frugally dressed. A man driving a Porsche, Jaguar, or Bentley is a greater turn-on than one driving an ordinary automobile. And this is not related to money. Such "status symbols" are merely visible indicators of the man's social competitiveness and power. This is an evolutionary reassurance that he is a safe and desirable partner; he will be good to have children with.

For the same reason, men prefer women who appear youthful, a clue to their ability to have babies. Males, from the perspective of evolution, ary scientists, want to spread their "seed" widely and father as many offspring as possible in order to have dominance over the clan. As a result, any hint of fertility and the potential for safely carry, ing a pregnancy on the woman's part turns them on. A narrow waist appeals because it "enlarges" the size of the hips and the pelvis. A face with large eyes and high cheekbones is attractive be, cause these features are signs of high estrogen levels. The capacity to "read" these signs is a silent but powerful legacy of male evolutionary history. This preference is "hardwired" in the male brain and operates outside of conscious awareness.

This affects what men regard as sexy things. They like female clothes that squeeze women's waists and show a little cleavage because such features give hints of women's youthfulness and potential fertility. Indeed, the entire cosmetic in, dustry for women is geared to provide men such clues. Women apply blush on their cheekbones and tweeze their eyebrows to heighten features that make them appear childlike on the one hand and simply youthful on the other. The former mo, bilizes a nurturing response in men and the latter an "impregnating" impulse; combined, the two result in a powerful feeling of sexual attraction. Women's cosmetic paraphernalia is what *men's* sexy things are about.

And if such arguments appear incredible, consider the suggestion of Desmond Morris, the author of *Naked Ape,* that when the quadraped apes evolved into our ancestors with upright locomotion, the sight of bulbous and pink female genitals was lost to the sight of the male ape. To compensate for this, lips on the faces of biped apes became everted and, with advancing civilization, methods were developed—like lipstick—to highlight their coloration so that males would be vaguely reminded of female genitalia.

Two cultural shifts

The psychoanalytic and evolutionary perspectives explain much about what men and women regard as "sexy things." However, they leave some conceptual nooks and crannies in this realm unexplained. Cultural shifts in the separation or amalgamation of gender characteristics especially get ignored in this regard. There are cultures where male and female roles are sharply demarcated, and there have been times in our own culture when this was the case. In such settings, "sexy things" for men and women are clearly distinct from each other. However, in cultural environments where gender roles are not so clear-cut, what is found sexy by men and what is found sexy by women become more or less indistinct.

In recent times, there are two notable examples of how male and female "sexy things" can become conflated. First, the heightened interest of men in how they dress seems to have resulted from the gay movement, whereby men themselves became the object of erotic gaze. Let me hasten to acknowledge that from Louis XIV to the dandy of Beau Brummel's day to the "power suit" of the 1980s, men have had an interest in fashion. However, this was largely to assert status and power. The current trend whereby men from all walks of life have become sartorially conscious is, to my mind, a byproduct of the gay movement. In other words, it is when the homosexual lifestyle became more socially acceptable that men's need to look good in order to be attractive also became evident. And it is by emulating targets of homosexual male gaze that the heterosexual acquired the tendency to dress better and amass "handsomizing" accoutrements. The hit television show *Queer Eye for the Straight Guy* makes this point in a truly astute manner.

A second cultural shift involves the relative softening of boundaries between what is regarded as typically "masculine" and "feminine." The economically fueled need for both males and females to share in child-rearing responsibilities has led to a greater usefulness—and hence acceptance—of the maternal or "feminine" attributes of men. Similar pressures have led to women shedding some of their traditional timidity and taking on more competitive and "masculine" attributes. Moreover, children are being raised in an increasingly gender-ambiguous world. All this has a growing impact upon the physical objects the two sexes use to enhance their attractiveness to each other. More than ever before, male and female "sexy things" might be on the way to becoming less distinct from each other. The resulting confusion is, however, a far lesser conundrum than we are about to encounter now.

Spicy, kinky, or creepy?

While contemporary mores have pushed the boundaries of acceptable sexual practices considerably, there are acts most would agree to be unacceptable. Such acts usually involve nonconsenting partners or the use of violence for sexual purposes. Examples of the former include pedophilia, bestiality, and necrophilia (sex with children, animals, and corpses, respectively). Examples of the latter include various forms of sexual sadomasochism, including whipping, paddling, spanking, piercing, cutting, hanging, stretching on racks, imprisonment in closets and boxes, hair pulling, nipple pinching, mummification, sexual asphyxiation, burning with cigarettes and cigarette lighters, dripping hot wax on genitals, ankle and wrist slashing, boot licking, diaper cuddling, feces smearing, and so on.

Physical objects are utilized in almost all these practices. Far from the relatively benign entity of sexual fetishism (where a man is turned on by a woman's shoes or needs her to wear an earring in order to maintain his erection), the sexual acts listed above are replete with mechanical paraphernalia of hostile eroticism: stretching racks, testicle and nipple pinchers, whipping chains and belts, mechanical spanking apparatuses (like Robospanker), and harnesses and bondage equipment of all sorts are only a few among the manmade objects for "outlying" sexual turnons.

Even when they do not involve explicit violence, some of the contraptions invented for sexual gratification have a frightening and bizarre quality. Click on to www.fuckingmachines.com and you will see what I am talking about. A selected listing of items available there include the Fucksall, the Tit Sucker, the Portafuck, the Fucking Chair, the Concrete Vibrator, and the curiously named Goat Milker, which happens to be a one-sixteenth-horsepower machine that provides a sensual pulsating suction of nipples. The ever forthright Web site includes among its weaknesses the following: "Can only suck nipples, not entire breast. Can not be used on clitoris."

The encounter with the relatively harsh and "gruesome" accoutrements on www.fuckingma chines.com makes one aware that some of these things are less about sexual release than about the discharge of hostility. While some might find the distinction prudish, it seems to me that these are apparatuses of "fucking" and not of making love. The quantum of force and aggression ever present in the act of lovemaking has exceeded its usual limit here. "Sexy things" of this type are actually "aggressive things" at their base.

Ordinary objects of day-to-day life can also be-come "sexy things" of the same type. The aggres-sive intent in their use is often subtle and hidden. For instance, those who insert things in their anus and rectum are on the surface looking for plea-sure. However, the very fact that objects intended for entirely different purposes are inserted in one's anus is in itself an act of hostility. Take a look at the list of foreign objects found in the anal canal compiled by surgeons D. B. Busch and J. R. Star-ling and you will get my point. Their list includes: lightbulb, apple, banana, cucumber, axe handle, dildo, spoon, flashlight, candle, pen, toothbrush, tennis ball, baby powder can, snuffbox, cold cream jar, keys, tobacco pouch, and beer glass. Inserting such objects into one's anus is a travesty of the purposes for which these objects are made. This constitutes an attack, however removed from con‹ scious awareness it might be, upon the established order of things. It is hostile in its essence.

In contrast are the "minor" and, more or less, day‹ to‹day deviations from conventional sexuality. They too employ physical objects. Fetishistic objects (e.g., high‹heeled shoes, dangling earrings) that some men need for maintaining an erection and dildos that some women use for masturbatory or lesbian sex constitute such things. Clothes, when used in a par‹ ticular way, can also belong in this category. The two vestimentary perversions illustrate this. The better known among them is *transvestism,* in which put‹ ting on the clothes of the opposite sex blurs gender differences between the sexes and creates erotic stimulation. The other is *homovestism,* in which the habitual wearing of slightly oversized or overdeco‹ rous clothes of the same gender makes one feel "turned on." The purpose of all these objects (fetishes, dildos, and sexually exciting clothes) is to assuage anxiety regarding the sexual differences between men and women. By and large, their intent is to blur gender differences and thus reduce the nervousness ordinarily associated with the perfor‑ mance of a sexual act. Such "sexy things" are meant to protect one against anxiety. They differ from the harsh mechanical tools of serious sexual perversions. The latter are conduits of hostility disguised as erotic excitement.

But wait. If one type of sexy thing is related to anxiety reduction and the other to discharging hostility, where does this leave us? Is there nothing that is purely "sexy"?

Climax

In order to answer this, consider:

- *From a psychoanalytic viewpoint,* "sexy things" are intended to provide a sense of safety so that one can overcome the nervousness associated with performing the sexual act.

- *From an evolutionary stance,* "sexy things" are conduits to genetically desirable mate selection and propagation of the species.

- *From a cultural perspective,* "sexy things" are tokens of accommodation to social trends defining gender roles and attractiveness.

- *Through a clinical lens,* which puts deviant sexuality at its center, "sexy things" are desperate though colorful masks for hostility.

None of these four perspectives sees "sexy things" as directly and exclusively related to sex. This leads one to the conclusion that "sexy things" are actually not about sex. In fact, there might not be such a thing as a sexy thing at all!

This brings to mind a tale often told among border patrolmen on the U.S./Mexico border. Fanciful and untrue though it most likely is, the tale is an instructive one. It goes like this. One day a U.S. patrolman sees a poor Mexican man standing close to the fence dividing the two countries. He has come on a bike and is holding a sack full of some soft material in his hand. The patrolman asks the Mexican, "What is in the bag?" "Dirt," the Mexican replies. The patrolman is not satisfied with this answer and asks him to open the bag. It turns out that the bag indeed contains nothing but dirt. The patrolman shrugs his shoulders and goes away. The next day, the Mexican guy shows up again on a bicycle with a sack full of dirt. The patrolman, suspecting that something is really up, once again asks that the sack be opened. And, once again, nothing but dirt is found in it.

This goes on day after day. The patrolman gets more and more irritated at the ritual. But he is also getting more confident that the day he does not check the contents of the bag, there will be cocaine—or some such thing—in it and the bag

will somehow be passed across the border. A smug-
gling scheme seems to be at work here. The patrolman decides never to give up. Never, never, never.

Each day this ritual is carried out between the
two men. Then, one day—after almost a year has
passed—exasperated and pulling his hair out, the
befuddled and embarrassed patrolman decides to
give up. He says to the Mexican, "Look, I will not
do anything, I promise. But please, for God's sake,
tell me what the hell it is that you have been doing
all this time." The Mexican, after seeking repeated
assurances that no punishment will come his way,
relaxes. He smiles and says, "I have been smug-
gling bicycles."

hybrid things

September 1956.

I am ten years old and am at the movies watching a crime thriller with my brother. The movie, called *C.I.D.* (the abbreviation for the Indian police's Criminal Investigation Division), is nearing its climax. The hero, who is an undercover cop, feigns illness in order to lure the villain to the closely guarded quarters of a hospital where he is purportedly admitted. The villain cannot resist the temptation. But he is clever. He fakes a limp and enters the hospital with a walking stick. He appears unarmed. Approaching the hero's bed, however, he suddenly pulls out a sword that was hidden in his hollow walking stick. The audience gasps. Terrified, I grab my brother's hand. Thankfully, the hero is not in his bed but hiding behind the door of the room. The hero pounces. A fight ensues and the villain is subdued. In the next scene, an unscathed and triumphant hero is enfolded in the arms of the heroine. The movie ends. We leave the theater and head home.

Within an hour or so, I recover from the shock of seeing the hero nearly getting killed. What does not leave me is the newly found awareness that certain physical objects can perform more than one function at the same time. The walking stick with a hidden sword becomes my introduction to the world of hybrid things. I am ten years old. My world is small and my thoughts go no further than tomorrow's homework or the next fun thing I can do with my brother or my cousins. I have no idea that what I have learned today about hybrid things will pop up in my writings some forty-eight years later.

What is a hybrid?

According to the dictionary definition, a hybrid is an offspring of two animals or plants of different races, breeds, varieties, or species. The mixing of two pure species, necessary for a hybrid to occur, may happen by accident or be artificially induced. However, hybrids can only occur when the species are closely enough related for the egg and the sperm to result in a viable embryo. Within the an⸍imal world, the best⸍known hybrid is the mule, a cross between a horse and a donkey. Far more curi⸍ous are feline hybrids. Bred primarily as novelties for public display, such animals include *ligers* (cross⸍breed between lions and tigers) and *leopons* (cross⸍breed between lions and leopards). Zebra⸍donkey hybrids (*zonkeys*) and whaledolphin hybrids (*wolphins*) are other examples of genetic admixture from the animal kingdom. While hybrid animals owe their existence to dual heredity, they are in⸍variably sterile themselves.

Hybrids also exist in the plant kingdom. Gar⸍deners and experimental botanists frequently cross⸍pollinate plants with aesthetic and scientific aims in mind. Perennial plants and evergreen trees are especially crossed with ease. The pursuit of ever more beautiful hues and shades of color has led to the creation of a vast array of hybrid flow⸍ers, especially roses and orchids. Examples of hy⸍brid grains and rare plants are also abundant.

While the concept of something being hybrid comes to us from the biological world, it is no less applicable to inanimate objects. Physical objects that are composed of diverse materials and have their origin in disparate technologies also qualify to be called "hybrid." A recent exhibition orga⸍nized by the Walker Arts Center in Minneapolis was devoted in its entirety to such objects. Included in the display called *Strangely Familiar* were garments that transformed into armchairs or kites, a ruler made of chocolate so that it could be eaten during school recess, and a house that could be folded up to fit in one's pocket. These extraordinary objects forced those who watched them to reconsider their basic relationship to the things around them. These objects opened up the "brave new world" of hybrid things.

Four types of inanimate mongrels

MULTIANCESTRAL OBJECTS. This category of hybrid objects is closest to the dictionary definition of the concept. It includes things that are heterogeneous in origin or composition. While the dramatic ones capture our attention, the fact is that numerous such things populate our living space. Examples of such daytoday multiancestral objects include a wood carving with ivory inlay, a turkey stuffed with pork, a martini or any other mixed drink, and an engagement ring made up of a South African diamond that is cut and polished in Belgium and affixed on a gold band from India. A more dramatic example of multiancestral objects are computers that have a combination of digital and analog systems or recent cars that run on both gas and electricity.

MULTIFUNCTIONAL OBJECTS. These are things that perform two (or more) separate func, tions, thus giving an illusion of belonging to two different classes of physical objects. The walking stick that hid a sword, mentioned in the beginning of my discussion, is an example of a multifunc, tional thing. More familiar objects of this type are children's pop,up books that transform printed pages into castles and dragons, convertible sofas that alternate between being a regular couch and a bed, and wristwatches with two faces so that one can simultaneously be oriented to two different time zones. TV and DVD "combos" as well as cell phones that can take pictures and send e,mails are recent additions to this category.

MULTIFORMAL OBJECTS. These are ob, jects that can readily change shape and reconfig, ure themselves. Such mutability is achieved either by making the object with a soft and malleable material or by what is called "modularity." The lat, ter consists of making the object in separate and independent modules that can snap into each other. At any time, a piece can be detached to alter the shape of the composite and to be used inde, pendently elsewhere. The most common example of this category is the sectional sofa with separate

pieces (e.g., chair, love seat, lounger) coming together to form the desired configuration. A more
dramatic illustration of multiformal hybrids is the
"Mutant Vase" created by the designer Anthony
Di Bitonto. The flower vase he designed locks a
steel coil between the walls of soft aluminum; it
can hold water while its wriggling coil permits one
to change its shape at any time.

MULTICONTEXTUAL OBJECTS. This type
of hybrid object aims to create a new and previously unintended use of a familiar object. By rele-
gating a new chore and new responsibility to the
ordinary object, multicontextual things embellish
its functional résumé and broaden the context of its
use. A book used as a paperweight and a folded
newspaper used as a fan during hot weather are
commonplace efforts in the direction of multifunc-
tionality (i.e., one object serving more than one
purpose). However, this is not what I have in mind
when talking of multicontextual objects. What I
mean by a multicontextual object is a thing that
does only what it is supposed to do, but it performs
that particular function in a way that enlarges its
context. An example is constituted by the "Hello
Coaster for Two" created by the industrial designer
Giovanni Pellone. In coming up with this product,
Pellone thought of drinking as a social ritual and a
cocktail party as a place where people meet in a

friendly and relaxed atmosphere. As a result, he de-signed a coaster for two glasses. Sharing a coaster might lead to sharing thoughts and feelings, he ar-gued. What was merely a humble place mat for one person's glass was thus transformed into a device to stimulate social interaction.

A less festive example is the highly unusual use of ostrich eggs by a New Zealand woman. She hollows them out, decorates them with semiprecious stones, and then sells them as "natural urns" for cremated remains. Each such egg sells for about $1,200. The harbinger of life thus becomes a container of death.

Together these four types of things (*multiancestral, multifunctional, multiformal,* and *multicontextual*) constitute the world of hybrid inanimate objects. The fact that they represent the post-industrial aspirations of man should, however, not make us overlook that the creation of hybrids has fascinated man from the dawn of civilization.

Centaurs, minotaurs, and mermaids

Going from a car that runs on both gas and electric-ity or a watch that tells time for two different regions simultaneously to legendary creatures with part-human and part-animal features might appear too big a leap at first glance. But if one looks carefully, the

hybrid technology of modern times and the fan-
tasied man-animal conflation of ancient myths turn
out to have many common characteristics. Before
going into these, however, I want to list some of the
better-known imaginary hybrid creatures.

- *Centaurs:* creatures from Greek mythology that
  were half-man and half-horse. They had a
  fondness for wine and a reputation for carrying
  off helpless maidens. Alleged to roam in the
  mountains of Thessaly, centaurs might have
  been the fanciful elaboration of the wild
  horsemen of prehistoric Asia, who often raided
  rural areas in Mittleeurope.

- *Minotaurs:* fabled creatures that were half-bull
  and half-man (sometimes with the head of a bull
  and the body of a man and sometimes the other
  way around). The first minotaur, according to
  Greek mythology, was born when Poseidon, who
  was mad at King Minos, arranged for a bull to
  have intercourse with Minos's wife, Pasiphae.

- *Mermaids:* living in the ocean, these creatures
  have the body of a woman above the waist and
  that of a fish from the waist down. According to
  the Irish legend, mermaids were pagan women
  banished from Earth by St. Patrick. (Less known
  are their male counterparts, called *Mermen.*)

- *Griffins:* mythical animals having the head,
  upper body, and wings of an eagle and the lower

body, hind legs, and tail of a lion. Such animals exist in both Indian and Greek mythologies and are seen as guardians of buried treasures.

- *Harpy:* a foul and rather malicious character from Greek mythology that is half-woman and half-bird. It was associated with the dark underworld of ghosts and demons.

- *Basilisk:* an imaginary serpent with a cock's or a man's head. It allegedly could kill simply by looking at someone. The fatal glance could, however, be turned upon itself. The way to kill a Basilisk therefore was to show it a mirror.

- *Satyrs and nymphs:* Greek mythological creatures with the upper half of their bodies being that of a goat and the lower half that of a man or a woman, respectively. Satyrs and nymphs are associated with debauchery. Indeed, the quasi-medical terms for male and female sexual voraciousness are satyriasis and nymphomania, respectively.

Hybrid creatures are found frequently in the world of religion, too. Among the most prominent examples are the following:

- *Ganesha:* a Hindu icon with the head of an elephant and the body of a boy. Worshipped by Hindus all over the world, the deity is regarded as especially auspicious for new beginnings.

- *Anubis:* a religious deity from the ancient Egyptian pantheon that had the head of a dog or a jackal and the body of a man. It was supposed to lead the dead to their final judgment.

What do these ancient flights of human imagination have to do with the inventive playfulness of modern technology? The first common characteristic between the fantastic creatures just described and machines that can perform multiple functions is the vibrant play of imagination. The creator of a mermaid or a minotaur, for instance, and the inventor of a hybrid car have both dared to think outside the proverbial box. They have broken established norms and pushed the envelope of possibility.

A second commonality between them lies in their rendering an object truly versatile. Why have two things when one thing can perform two functions? The mythmaker and the inventor are in the pursuit of functional economy above all. The former creates a visual icon or tale that cryptically contains multiple aspects of human striving. The latter makes a machine that performs the functions of two or more machines. What both of them accomplish does "more" but uses means that are actually "less." The attempted synthesis of "more" and "less" propels their generative impulse.

OBJECTS *of* *our* DESIRE

Finally, the fabulist and the engineer both act as "therapists" for mankind. In his own way, each provides a solution to difficult emotions we struggle with all the time. For example, you are involved in a long-distance relationship and have to figure out what time is it where your lover is each time you have to call him on the phone. The time gap and the necessity to remind yourself of it is a hassle. All right. We will make a watch with two dials, one that shows the time here and the other that shows the time there. Now you are in touch with time in two separate zones. You can almost imagine what the person you love in the other time zone is doing. Your pain of separation is lessened.

Now take another example. You are overrun with sexual impulses, but being greedy in the realm of sex does not fit the nice and civil image you have of yourself. No problem. We will come up with the Satyr, a half-man and half-goat creature full of lust, so that you can vicariously enjoy your fantasies of sexual excess while simultaneously devaluing them by attributing them to an animal (or an "animal" part of yourself). Satisfied?

The point I am trying to make through all this is that the invention of a hybrid product, regardless of it being in the realm of mythology or technology, is invariably bold on the creative front, economical on the functional front, and exhilarating on the emotional front. It captures what is the most pure, wide-eyed, and childlike in us. It says that elements that seemed incompatible can actually be combined to beneficial effect. It reminds us that more is possible and that the constituents of novelty are at our disposal all the time.

This is not to say that such inventiveness never meets disastrous results. Indeed it does. An example is Kaboom! The Suicide Bomber Game, released in late 2002 on NewGrounds.com, a game and animation Web site. Using a mouse, the player of this game moves a suicide bomber through a crowded marketplace and then, with a click, has him blow up innocent bystanders. Points are awarded to the player according to the number of people killed. Besides being tasteless, the game trivializes terrorist violence and the political tragedies that cause and result from it. A multicontextual object to be sure, Kaboom extends the youthful pleasure of video games to wanton murder. And this is done for prurient monetary interests.

Not motivated by such greed and certainly a little less dark are the geometrically defiant etchings of M. C. Escher (1898–1972). Forcing roof-supporting columns from one side of the room to merge with ceiling at the opposite end, making waterfalls run against gravity, and changing fish into birds, the Dutch artist constantly challenged the limits of formal possibility. His most outstanding gesture of creative defiance involved raising the question of why God had not created an animal with wheels. Drunk with megalomanic talent, Escher set out to design such an animal himself and, in the process, produced some striking drawings.

The mythmaking inherent in the search for hy‹ brid objects does not, however, have to be omi‹ nous or mad. It can have a sunny disposition like the 1980s toys called Transformers, which came in the form of trucks or cars that with a few shifts of the pieces could be changed into human char‹ acters. Mixing animate and inanimate together and creating space for the playful imagination, such objects reflect our most innocent and sub‹ lime childhood efforts at grappling with our inner and outer worlds. Billy Collins, a former Poet Lau‹ reate of the United States, captures the flickering beauty of such moments in his poem "Creatures":

> Hamlet noticed them in the shape of clouds
> but I saw them in the furniture of childhood
> creatures trapped under surfaces of wood,
> one submerged in a polished sideboard,
> one frowning from a chair‹back,
> another howling from my mother's silent
>   bureau,
> locked in the grain of maple, frozen in oak.

Our emotional reactions
to hybrid things

What Collins does with effortless grace is to open the door to a universe of imagination where inter‚ mingling and merger replace dry separateness and categorization of ideas. He offers us a world in which fluid shifts take place across set divisions and new configurations appear on the horizon. Rabbits pop out of hats and Jack does not stay in the box. Bones are changed into blood and conti‚ nents into ocean. A walking stick reveals a sword and an ostrich egg becomes a cremation urn. This is the world of hybrid things.

In this world, we constantly witness seemingly disparate things function harmoniously together. Such experience exerts a reassuring and optimistic effect upon us. If the digital and analog system, and gas and electricity, can work in unison, per‚ haps the ill‚fitting parts of our daily lives and even our inner selves can someday come together as well. The encounter with a hybrid object offers us hope. Let us be honest. All of us have contradictory propensities in ourselves. Duality is built in our na‚ ture. Animal‚human, child‚adult, moral‚immoral, feminine‚masculine, offspring‚parent, public‚private, and many other splits characterize our existence. We strive for integration, hoping that being less di‚

vided will bring us peace. We seek the sutures of social bonds, the ointment of religion, and the elixir of psychotherapy to bring about such inner integration. And we are fortunate that our cultural institutions offer us fairy tales, poetry, art, and other creative avenues to find imaginative bridges across our inner lacerations. Encounter with hybrid things is a bridge of this very sort. Hybrid objects embody a symphony of collaboration and we merrily join in the "sing-along"!

There is also something inherently transcendent about hybrid objects. They offer the promise of new and creative solutions for old problems. Feeling hot in a place that's not air-conditioned? You don't have to continue suffering. The newspaper you have been carrying offers to become a fan. Getting drowsy in a train but have no pillow? Well, the laptop wrapped up in your jacket would become a pillow right away. Getting bored by looking day after day at the same sofa? Try sectional seating. You can have a different configuration every week. Let me put it flatly: hybrid objects make us happy because they open up new vistas for imagination.

But don't hybrid objects inherently destroy the established order of things? Don't they alter what was originally there and thus make it disappear? Indeed, they do. And therefore they can be perceived as threatening by those who like old and estab-lished conventions. Try selling a contemporary sectional sofa to one who adores the somber stabil-ity of Victorian decor and you will get my point.

The matter is, however, more serious than this. The world around us is undergoing a transforma-tion the likes of which it has never before experi-enced. Migration between countries has reached very high proportions. Globalization through free-market enterprise and cultural diffusion via the Internet have resulted in a threat to the tribal, re-gional, and religious identities of people all over the world. We are entering the era of hybrid people and hybrid cultures. What feelings does that arouse in us?

Hybridization versus fundamentalism

It might appear curious to start with clocks and cars and end up with bicultural and hybrid identities of migrants and "globalized" people. But the similarity is staring us in the face and cannot be denied. We can hardly ignore that in the same way a hybrid physical object is made up of diverse sources, the personal identities of more and more people in to-day's world are evolved from diverse lines of hered-ity, race, religion, ethnicity, and national origin.

Discrete tribes and stolid regional cultures are fast becoming a thing of the past. World languages are getting mixed up with one another, and while English is emerging as the universal lingua franca, its own character has changed due to increasing assimilation of new lexical streams. Intercultural marriages are becoming common, and the offspring of such unions invariably carries the imprint of two different traditions at its psychic core. Migration across nations is at its highest, and the transformative impact it has on the self-experience and outward behavior of the individual has become undeniable.

Similar hybridization is visible at the functional level. To be sure, Jewish doctors, Hindu mystics, WASP golf players, and black athletes are still around. But the rigid social divisions that spurred such stereotypes have not been able to sustain the momentum of the changing world around them. We now see Arabs working as stand-up comedians in Hollywood, Hindu Brahman entrepreneurs on Wall Street, the milk-white followers of the Hare Krishna movement, and so on. Jobs on the IT market are increasingly "outsourced" to India, and handmade rugs from that country as well as from Iran and Pakistan adorn more and more suburban houses in the United States. The Internet has created a universal forum for information dispatch as well as for all sorts of formal and informal dialogue between people. Cell phones and e-mail have become ready-made electronic tethers for people separated by mountains, deserts, and oceans. And all this is having a powerful homogenizing impact upon the world culture.

As some celebrate such transformation of our previously compartmentalized world into a global village, others cling to old maps for social conduct. They retrospectively embellish the accounts of the past and feel threatened by the present state of affairs. The ideal future for them is a replication of the "glorious" past. Attempting to stop the passage of time, they prefer a rosary over a calculator and a horoscope over a stethoscope. More problematically, they place belief over knowledge and "divine" wisdom over learned truths. Dilution of culture is a mortal sin for them. In the name of purity, they abhor any threat to the established order even if it promises to improve matters for all concerned.

Both these tendencies (globalization and fundamentalism) are on the rise throughout the world. Christians, Muslims, Hindus, and Jews are all affected by this tumultuous paradox of our times. Each group is melting into the neighboring other and, in the process, losing its moorings in history and tradition. Each shows signs of becoming hybrid.

And, as a recoil to this development, each is manifesting the resurgence of orthodoxy and regressive search for purity. No wonder polarized camps of hybridization and fundamentalism have sprung up everywhere. One can only hope that the synthesis of these diverse ideologies might yield pathways toward a future that is based upon the present and is not entirely divorced from the past. Donald Winnicott's celebrated phrase "There is no originality except on the basis of tradition" comes to mind in this context. The question, however, remains whether the purists can ever see it this way.

A different sort of walking stick

I am twelve years old.

The memory of the dreaded walking stick I had seen two years earlier on a celluloid screen has all but disappeared from my mind. I am on a bus that is taking twenty or so schoolkids for a two-week trip to Nainital, a beautiful mountain resort in northern India. We stop for lunch in Haldwani, an obscure village some four thousand feet above sea level. The teacher who is accompanying us gives us a fifteen-minute "recess" to look around before resuming the sojourn. I walk over to a nearby shop, which is selling things made of wood: bowls, tables, jewelry boxes, and similar objects. As I wander through the shop, I come across a walking stick, sturdy and smooth, with an intricately carved lion's-head handle. I immediately know that I want to buy it for my grandfather. He has a number of walking sticks already, but I know he'll be delighted to add this one to his collection. I purchase it with my pocket money for the trip.

Over the next two weeks, I keep the walking stick with me. It provides me a sense of comfort. Having it by my side makes me feel as if I am in the strong and protective company of my grand-father. The lion's head that is carved on its handle becomes a smiling teddy bear as the night falls on the summer camp. Made to assist an old man walk, the walking stick now helps a young boy fall asleep. Like its evil twin—the one with a hidden sword—this walking stick is also a hybrid object. The dif-ference, of course, is that the hidden element is intangible and pertains not to hate but to love.

fake things

Pink, glistening, and, frankly, a bit intimidating—I never could muster the courage to touch them—is how my grandfather's dentures appeared to me.

They were semicircular structures made of wax or plastic with a built-in roof for a palate, neatly interrupted by pearly white teeth. My grandfather would take them out of his mouth from time to time and put them in a glass of water or simply on the table next to his armchair. As a nine- or ten-year-old boy, I would catch myself looking at them intently. Something about them was inviting and something about them was slightly unnerving. To this day, I have not figured out what gave rise to the opposing feelings. What I do remember clearly is the palpable increase in my uneasiness at the moment when he would put them in his mouth, usually right before a meal. Watching him put the dentures into his mouth made me uneasy. Having never seen anybody put anything in his mouth and not eat it, I feared that he might swallow them. The fact that he never did was certainly reassuring, but the relief lasted only till the next time he reached out to place the dentures in his mouth.

The encounter with my grandfather's dentures was my first exposure to something that was *naqli* (the word for "artificial" in my mother tongue, Urdu) and yet played a significant role in life. This might seem a bit peculiar. After all, aren't most things artificial? Chairs, clocks, forks and knives, ties, shoes, electric razors, and all such things are man-made, hence "artificial" by definition. But I am using the designation "artificial things" in a more specific and narrow sense, referring to objects that are purposely made to replace natural things.

As I grew older and my life experience widened, especially in the course of becoming a medical doctor, I witnessed the helpful role of more and more artificial things in man's life. These ranged from metallic knee joints and glass eyes to steel-made skull plates and latex balloons inserted in coronary arteries. Artificial things, it seemed, did not have to oppose the natural order. They could cooperate with nature and help sustain its intended goals for us. Medical specialties of all sorts and especially orthopedics and plastic surgery seemed to rely on such useful phantoms all the time. I came to accept the place of *naqli,* or artificial, things in physical life just as I learned good manners, which had also appeared sort of artificial in the beginning to me. All was well till I came across the word *jaali* in my mother tongue. *Jaali,* which meant "fake," puzzled me greatly. I felt an urgent need to sort out the difference between *naqli* and *jaali* or, to put it in English, between "artificial" and "fake." And yet it took nearly five decades before I was able to give the matter serious consideration.

Artificial versus fake things

The difference between an "artificial" thing and a "fake" thing exists on three levels. First and foremost, the artificial thing openly acknowledges its synthetic nature. A prosthetic limb or a glass eye, for instance, makes no claim to be a real extremity or eye, respectively. As existential entities, such objects are fundamentally "honest." Fake things, in contrast, have deception built in at their core. A counterfeit dollar bill wishes to pass as the real thing. A forged signature aims to achieve legal authority comparable to the actual inscription. Unlike an artificial thing, which says, "Accept me for what I am," a fake thing says, "I will not reveal my real nature to you."

Another difference between artificial and fake things lies in who draws benefit from them. Artificial things are intended to benefit their users. This is as true of biomedical accoutrements as it is of replicas and reproductions of arts and antiques. A person using a prosthetic limb gains lost bodily function and this enhances his self-esteem. He feels happier. The individual who adorns a wall of her house with a reprint of Van Gogh's *Starry Night* or keeps a little replica of the Eiffel Tower in her curio cabinet is no different. She fully recognizes these objects as copies of the original but still derives pleasure from them. The same is true of the one who buys reproduction antique furniture. He is aware of his chairs and tables being replicas and yet enjoys the illusion of the bygone era they represent. Acceptance of artificiality is accompanied by the plebian comfort of borrowed greatness in all these instances. All in all, such goods benefit the one who buys them.

In contrast, fake things are intended solely for the benefit of their producers and sellers. Who gains from making counterfeit currency or forged antiquities? Who reaps the benefit of selling false originals of rare manuscripts? The fact is that the buyer of such products suffers not only monetary loss but shame over her own gullibility. She is pushed through a door of naïveté into the chamber of helpless remorse. Contrary to such collapse of self-esteem on the buyer's part, the producer and/or seller of forgery obtains financial rewards and triumphant glee from the transaction.

Finally, artificial things (e.g., replicas, reprints, and reproductions) and fake things (e.g., counterfeit products and forgeries) are created with different emotional attitudes. Artificial things are constructed from an emotional position of respect and humility. One who makes a copy of Monet's *Water Lilies* or da Vinci's *Mona Lisa* clearly declares his admiration of these masters and his desire to emulate them. He acknowledges his being of lesser status than the master himself; after all, he is making a copy, not the original. He is an avowed fan, a pupil of sorts, an acolyte. Now compare this with the forger who, far from sitting at the feet of the master, claims comparable stature for himself. No wonder, he is arrogant, cocky, and full of himself. He may be a man of taste, but when all is said and done, he turns out to be a knowledgeable amateur and aesthete rather than an artist. His work lacks genuine submission to the tyranny of his craft, and his effort is in the service of cleverness. Like Oscar Wilde and Andy Warhol, he puts his genius into his life and his talent into his work.

Fake things, in essence, are lies in the form of physical objects. Their goal is to appear what they are not—namely, real. Deception runs in their veins and mendacity is their mother tongue. Matters, however, can become worse. Pretentious erudition can change into a smattering of fanciful words and false creativity into outright forgery.

A box containing divine bones

In the spring of 2002, archaeologists, theologians, antique dealers, and journalists from all over the world were stunned by the "discovery" of an ancient limestone box that purportedly had contained the bones of James, the brother of Jesus Christ. The French scholar Andre Lamaire, who reported the find in *Biblical Archaeology Review,* was convinced of its authenticity. Such an ossuary ("bone box") was used to store bones in Jewish burial practices of the time; the skeletal remains of the dead were collected a year or so after the burial and placed into a limestone box with a lid. The discovery of James's ossuary was of immense religious and historical significance. Not surprisingly, it attracted worldwide attention of both a credulous and a skeptical variety. Debates raged in scholarly journals over the veracity of the claim, and archaeological sleuths of all stripes took out their magnifying glasses. The *Geological Survey of Israel* and the *Israeli Antiquities Authority* also decided to enter the arena.

It turned out that the "ancient" artifact was actually a modern forgery. Many of its features did not hold up to serious scrutiny. For instance, while the decorations on the box were effaced and pitted, the inscription declaring it to be James's ossuary was in letters with youthfully sharp edges. Moreover, the limestone erosion caused by bacteria over time *(biovermiculation)* did not extend to the engraved letters, suggesting that these were added later on. Doubt on the box's authenticity was also cast by the difficulty in tracing the detailed origins of its discovery.

That story is in itself quite intriguing. It turns out that Andre Lamaire had learned of it from a collector named Oded Golan, whom he had met in a Jerusalem market by chance. Golan, a Tel Aviv engineer and entrepreneur, said that he had something of interest to Lamaire, and among these objects was the James ossuary. But where did Golan get it from? Well, according to Golan, he bought the thing in the Old City from an Arab antique dealer nearly thirty years ago. And there is no trace of that Arab dealer anywhere! As you can imagine, this made the tale told by Golan hard to swallow. Put this alongside the fact that he would not allow the bone fragments he claimed to have taken out of the ossuary to be displayed or analyzed. According to him, these are stored at his home in a Tupperware container!

What motivates someone to create a forgery?

Oded Golan is currently under police investigation in Israel with charges of forgery and intent to deceive others. His life story is a script for a made-for-TV movie. But he is not alone in the large and worldwide cadre of forgers and counterfeiters who claim to have "discovered" amazing antiquities and "created" great pieces of art. What makes them do it? What makes anyone pass off an inauthentic product as authentic? Why do people cheat?

On the surface, the answer to such questions is simple. One look at the exorbitant prices successful forgeries in the realm of art can fetch and you know that monetary benefit is a major motivation for such "creativity of deception." Now, you and I know that before art became commercialized, reproducing the work of a master was considered a sign of respect, not a forgery. Copies were recognized as such and financial gain did not motivate their production. It is with the Renaissance, when the interest in cultural antiquities raised the monetary value of art, that the trend toward passing off such "copies" as real began. There was money to be made by such forgery.

The list of those who thrived in this business is indeed long. Two outstanding art forgers who made enormous money by their deceptive craft are Hans van Meegeren (1889–1947), the Dutch art dealer who painted many fake Vermeers, and Tom Keating (1917–1984), the British con artist who forged more than two thousand paintings by more than one hundred artists in his lifetime. The fact, however, is that the money made by these two master forgers constitutes a minuscule proportion of that made by art forgers all over the world. And art is not the only arena where plausible fake products offer lucrative financial rewards. Collectors of autographs, rare manuscripts, old photographs, letters, and even stamps and coins know very well how widely inauthentic objects circulate in the bazaars of their passion. They can also recount all sorts of tales involving someone being swindled by a forger who got away with a huge sum of money.

Bruce Gimelson, who is a dealer and a collector in Garrison, New York, contends that fakes are an increasing problem in his business, as the Internet is causing a glut of dubious material to hit the market. He goes on to say:

> Counterfeits and fakes are getting to be a worse and worse problem with the unfettered sales over the Internet. I'd say I see a hundred times more fake Babe Ruths and Lou Gehrigs than I saw in the old days. Sitting Bull is also big with the fakers. The Beatles, too. It's just astonishing what is going out for sale these days. Recently, another dealer e-mailed me pictures of an autograph he was selling. It was signed Humpty Bogert (instead of Humphrey Bogart). I mean it's incredible.

Most such fakery is intended to make a quick buck. However, monetary profit is not the only motive for creating a forgery. Emotional factors also seem to play a role here. Prominent among these are the following:

- Creating a "successful" forgery affords one the wicked pleasure of fooling others. Compared to oneself, others now appear silly and stupid. One comes across as smart, others dumb. The sadistic triumph over their innocence results in gleeful mocking. It promises to undo the chronic feelings of inferiority and impotence the forger often carries within himself.

- Trading in fake products invariably involves a rebellion against ordinary morality. It involves breaking the law as well. Making and selling counterfeit objects can thus give vent to emotional conflicts with authority figures. The irreverence and bravado of an impostor is a slap in the face of the established order. The ever-present risk of being caught adds to the thrill of defiance.

- Fakery also fulfills strivings for magical powers. To produce a dollar bill in one's basement, for instance, gratifies our childish wishes for becoming "rich" pronto. To paint a Cézanne or a Picasso over a few days in downtown Cleveland is to reverse time, change location, and acquire creative genius at will. Just like that, with a snap of the fingers. Feels good, doesn't it?

Such considerations of the forger's sentiments bring us to the other side of the equation, namely the emotional responses of the witness of a forgery. As victims of forgery, we feel an admixture of outrage and shame. We are hurt by the betrayal and embarrassed by our gullibility. All this I have already talked about to you. Now I want to tackle the emotions aroused in us when we are mere witnesses or onlookers of a forgery, not its victim. Believe me, even under such "benign" circumstances, our responses are not simple. We experience a mixture of emotions that reveal some very fundamental things about our nature as "civilized" human beings. More

important, these emotions indicate that, unbe-
known to us, a conspiracy might exist between us
and the producer of imposturous goods. We might
be his accomplice, or he ours. But before going into
all of this, I want to tell you about a famous forger.
My hope is that this encounter will emotionally
"prime" you for the disturbing revelation to follow.

Introducing Joseph Cosey

Born in 1887 in Syracuse, New York, Joseph Cosey
was probably the most notorious twentieth-century
forger in the United States. As a youngster, he was
in frequent trouble with the law and, upon joining
the army, was dishonorably discharged for as-
saulting a fellow soldier. His subsequent years were
characterized by a pattern of low-grade criminal behavior, including passing "bad" checks, adopting
false identities, shoplifting, and stealing. He was im-
prisoned many times during the course of these
events and was ultimately locked up in California's
San Quentin prison for ten years.

Such punishments failed to reform him, and in
1929 he began a remarkable career of forgery. This
was a rather dramatic turn of events. Cosey, who
was forty-two years old then, visited the Library of
Congress and viewed a document signed by Ben-
jamin Franklin in 1786. He stole it, but instead of

immediately reselling it, he used the document to help him imitate Franklin's handwriting. After some practice, he became adept at it and went on to sell many documents signed by "Franklin" to unsuspecting history buffs and autograph collectors.

The Web site of Courtroom Television Network, which covers Joseph Cosey's life in detail, reports that he reproduced the signatures of many other American legends, including George Washington, Thomas Jefferson, and Abraham Lincoln, as well as Mark Twain, Walt Whitman, and Edgar Allan Poe. These forgeries often went undetected since they were prepared with great care, using antiquated paper and truly old ink. Nonetheless, Cosey did get caught in 1937 while selling a letter purportedly written by Abraham Lincoln. The eternal youthfulness of Casey's handwriting, while those he was imitating showed age-related changes in theirs, and the slipup of using a steel nib, which had not been invented at the time the document was allegedly written, landed him back in jail.

Joseph Cosey died in 1953, a seventy-year-old heirless pauper. He is no more, but experts believe that many of his forged documents are perhaps still on display in museums. More impressive is the fact that Cosey's known forgeries have themselves become collector's items. The deceptions he peddled with cunning are now proudly displayed by honest citizens in their homes. What more could the unrepentant con artist have wanted?

Our emotional reactions to forgeries

This brings up our emotional reactions to a forgery, which happen to be quite varied. Some responses are readily apparent to us; others emerge only after we have given the matter some thought and done some soul-searching.

We are all familiar with the scorn we feel upon seeing poorly made Barbie dolls from the Persian Gulf, French perfumes concocted in the Philippines, faux-pearl necklaces offered on QVC, fake Rolex watches sold on a New York City street corner, Coach handbags made in Guatemala, and designer-label clothes made in Bangladeshi sweatshops. We deride them. The scorn reflects our rejection of fraudulence in general. It helps us repudiate aspects of inauthenticity in our own personality makeup. It is as if by belittling fake products we are saying that we ourselves are entirely genuine in our day-to-day behavior. Our dislike of counterfeit goods thus turns out to be rather self-serving. This is a sort of fakery itself.

More embarrassing is the possibility that forgeries and counterfeit products provide vicarious gratification to our hidden, less‑than‑noble impulses. The childhood intolerance for the labor of effort and for the helplessness of waiting to become adept at something finds a secret ally in the pro‑ ducer of artifice. He fuels our suppressed longings for quick and swift results that are achieved with‑ out effort and practice. He tells us that the om‑ nipotence we have reluctantly renounced can find gratification after all. He offers us a path that does not traverse through law‑abiding territories of learning, practice, and hard work. And we gladly give in to his seductions. To put it bluntly, the clan‑ destine pact between us and the forger goes like this: "If this guy in Texas can paint a Van Gogh, maybe we too can accomplish great and even impossible feats. If he can break rules and fool others, maybe we can also do that which is prohib‑ ited to us." No wonder we feel a mixture of barely suppressed thrill and a delicious wave of guilty fear upon encountering a fake product. Hold a coun‑ terfeit hundred‑dollar bill in your hands and you will immediately know what I am talking about.

Something even deeper about human nature is revealed by the observation that we admire a better fake more than a sloppy fake. The more devilishly fooled we are, the more delight we take in the im‑ postor's product. Why is that? Is the pleasure of‑ fered us by a good fake merely aesthetic? In other words, do we like a better replica of Rodin's *Thinker* or of the Leaning Tower of Pisa because they "look" good, that is, closer to the original thing? Or is it because the better-executed fake shows more thoughtfulness and effort and, by implication, a greater amount of respect toward the creator of the original? The answer to both these questions is a resounding yes. Overtly, our reasons for reacting more favorably to a good fake are aesthetic. A replica that closely approximates the original stimulates the admiration we feel toward the latter. We like the sensation. Covertly, witnessing a good fake provides us a well-balanced compromise between our longings for magic on the one hand and the recognition of the value of effort on the other. It also provides a simultaneous gratification of our childhood wishes to outsmart our parents as well as to keep them on a higher level than us. Since all of us have the remnants of such childhood wishes in the basements of our minds, it is not surprising that we simply "love" a well-executed fake.

Gray areas

In my emphasis upon the devious and potentially sinister aspects of fake things, I do not want to overlook that some outright fake things also offer us a lot of fun. Monopoly money, Halloween costumes, movie sets and theater, and Mickey Mouse are perhaps the most prominent examples of how "fake" things can be profoundly entertaining. It relieves us, at least temporarily, from the burdens of reality. We can enter the less harsh world of illusion. Being responsible adults does not mean that we give up enjoying a good magic show. Fakeness, like French fries and television, is not all bad. The relief that passes over the face of a teenager's parent upon learning that the tattoo his offspring has just acquired is fake is a testimony to this point.

Moreover, the distinctions between real, artificial, and fake things are not as rigid as they seem. The fact is that a certain overlap between what is fake and what is authentic is not uncommon. A couple of instances readily come to mind. Remember the James ossuary mentioned earlier in this chapter? It was initially considered authentic, only to be later found a forgery. In contrast, the renowned Dutch painter Vermeer's *Young Woman Seated at the Virginals* had been treated as a forgery since 1947 but was declared to be genuine in March 2004. Besides such temporal shifts, a mixture of authenticity and inauthenticity pervades the material world around us. Sometimes this happens because fake and real things are interspersed, like the replica of a Colonial-era table on which sits the framed drawing made by your daughter when she was five years old. The former is "fake," the latter is real. At other times, the real-artificial-fake distinction is drowned by the very nature of a particular object. The cell-phone voice of a relative who lives hundreds of miles away, the photographs of deceased grandparents on the mantelpiece, and the somber portraits of distinguished alumni in the corridors of a law school are all such things. They contain elements of being real, artificial, and fake at the same time and often in indecipherable proportions. And our life, instead of becoming disjointed and confused, grows richer due to such benevolent illusions of reality.

nothing

misplacing, losing,
and letting go
of things

The suitcase is in my garage.

It sits among cardboard boxes, trash cans, crates of beer and Pepsi, ice shovels, bags full of old newspapers, a rickety ladder, and coils of inauthentically green gardening hose. Bluish gray, very heavy, locked. Leaning against the painted cinderblock wall for the last three years.

Here is its full story.

In the fall of 2001, my friend Pramod Bhatia decided to return to India for good. He was a loner and on principle avoided owning things. He did not buy a house nor did he own a car. His furniture and even his television set were rented. During his nearly fifteenyear stay in the United States, he acquired a bare minimum of things, as if he was forever ready to leave. So when the time came, all of his belongings fit inside two suitcases. He took one to India and left the other with me. He said he would come back in a year to pick it up. That was three years ago.

I hear from Pramod once in a while—an occasional e-mail, a rare phone call. He leads a reclusive life in a small hotel in the foothills of northern India. He never asks about the suitcase he left with me. I also avoid the topic, feeling vaguely uneasy about bringing it up.

As a friend, I keep his suitcase, telling myself that he might come back one day to retrieve it. As a psychoanalyst, I suspect he wishes to be permanently rid of it but lacks the willpower to actually discard it. So he arranges a situation whereby the thing, left behind for years, will sooner or later be dumped by its custodian. Pramod will then have "lost" his suitcase without having actually thrown it away. He will act earnestly disappointed, but in the deeper layers of his mind, he will be relieved. It is a sad game that people play with themselves. Believe me, you and I are not immune to it.

Separating from things can be so painful that we need to disguise our intentions. Saying goodbye is never easy, even if it is to inanimate partners of our lives. We suffer, make excuses, and use all sorts of "delay tactics." Life, however, forces us to part with our beloved possessions on a regular ba‹ sis. Sometimes this is due to external events that are out of our control. At other times we lose things by "misplacing" them.

Misplacing and losing things

One way of saying good‹bye to things is to simply "lose" them. Here the letting go of a thing takes place *before* we work through our feelings about the impending separation. Rather than deliber‹ ately renounce a thing, we make ourselves give it up first and deal with the mourning later. This usually happens when our feelings about a partic‹ ular object are conflicted.

For example, Myles Kane, a sixty‹year‹old insur‹ ance agent who had just celebrated his twenty‹fifth wedding anniversary, went to Miami for a work‹ related trip. He ended up having sex with an Italian woman tourist who was staying in the same hotel. The next morning, Myles felt guilty but kept this feeling suppressed throughout the day, during which he attended important business meetings. Vaguely uneasy, he nonetheless worked hard at facts and figures. Later that evening, as he was pack‹ ing his suitcase to catch a flight home, he could not find his wallet. He panicked. He searched the hotel room and went through the pockets of his suits.

Again and again, he called the restaurant where he had had lunch with his colleagues, but they did not have his wallet, either. He could not find it anywhere. It was lost. Or, shall we say, *he* had lost it.

Could it be that Myles's guilt about cheating on his wife caused him to punish himself by losing his money and credit cards? And the picture of his wife taken on their recent wedding anniversary that was in his wallet?

All instances of losing things do not have such dark dynamics. Often the loss is purely accidental, caused by our being rushed, inattentive, or preoccupied. Items left on subway trains—books, newspapers, lunch boxes, gloves, umbrellas—usually reflect this state of affairs. However, simply because we have no idea why we misplaced or lost something does not prove that the occurrence is devoid of deeper meaning. We might attribute our loss to "carelessness" without realizing that losing that thing was our mind's way of forcing us to say "goodbye" to it for one reason or another. Either, like Myles, we were feeling guilty about something and needed to punish ourselves by losing a valued object, or the role played by that object in our life was somehow over.

Maryanne O'Brien, an Irish Catholic schoolteacher, was actively pursued by Gary Kaplan, a Jewish clinical psychologist whom she had met while taking evening classes in Spanish. While flattered and even a bit "turned on," Maryanne did not want to start dating Gary. She feared that their religious backgrounds would preclude a more sustained involvement between them. At times she thought that she had seen Gary looking a little warily at the silver cross that she wore around her neck. She was not sure about it, though. Gary, however, was oblivious to her concerns. He was persistent, and his earnest overtures ultimately paid off. Maryanne's heart melted and she agreed to go out with him. Their first few dates went well. Gary was in seventh heaven. Maryanne was also happy. However, just around this time, she "misplaced" her cross and could not find it anywhere.

Both Myles and Maryanne "forced" themselves to give up things that mattered to them. Their subsequent distress was as much about the loss as it was about the fact that it happened "accidentally." This does not mean that we may not feel regret at having actively discarded something, thinking (wrongly, as it turns out!) that we are ready to let go of it.

Having finally broken up with her on-again, off-again boyfriend of nearly seven years, Carol Dunson decided to throw away the journals in which she had recorded the memories of their good and bad moments together. Years later, married and the mother of two, Carol occasionally regrets the decision. She loves her husband but lacks the aching desire she felt for her boyfriend of years ago. At times, she wishes that she could read her journal from that era again to see what all that was about. Her journal could inform her, and it hurts her that she got rid of it. "I feel I threw my soul away," she recently confided to a good friend.

Much greater distress is, however, felt by those who are forced by external circumstances to part with important things.

Being traumatically deprived of things

A number of situations cause us to part with things in a painful way. Divorce is one of them. The dissolution of a marriage shatters personal bonds and forces the couple to divide their possessions. These "marital assets"—homes, furniture, cars, artwork, family heirlooms, souvenirs and mementos, pots and pans, books, and all sorts of bric-a-brac—have an emotional significance beyond their monetary value. What was lovingly acquired is begrudgingly renounced, if not greedily and angrily held on to. Fights break out, bitter arguments and recriminations ensue, and lawyers are brought in to sort out the "property division" between a couple.

Even in the absence of such mutual bickering, separation from familiar objects during divorce can be acutely painful. Often it sets into motion rituals of farewell that are private and unnoticed by others.

Farrell Lines, a forty-nine-year-old cardiologist from suburban Chicago, had difficulty sleeping during the weeks before he left the home he shared with his soon-to-be ex-wife for good. Having fallen in love with another woman, he had filed for divorce from Dianne, his wife of nearly twenty years. As part of the property settlement, she would keep the house and its contents. While at one level Farrell felt good about this arrangement—it diminished his guilt at breaking up the marriage—he nonetheless was pained at the prospect of leaving behind the beautiful furniture, antiques, and artwork that he had laboriously collected over the years.

Late at night, with his wife fast asleep in the master bedroom, he would come out of his study and wander through their sprawling house. He would stop in the dining room, looking intently at the furniture there: the mahogany dining table, on which he and Dianne had hosted many dinners, the chairs, the buffet, the wine rack. All were soaked in memories. He would gently caress them. Moving on to the living room, Farrell encountered his beloved coffee table, made of cherry wood framing and a four-by-six slab of glass. The table's large size had always been vaguely reassuring to him, and now the thought of being separated from it brought his pent-up anguish to the surface. Farrell would begin to cry. He would pass his fingers over the table's surface, repeatedly feeling the turn of the wood at its four corners, as if to memorize it or leave something of himself behind in the darkness of the wood. The large oil painting of two dogs and a horse above the sofa would next capture his attention. The thought of parting from it was unbearable. He could vividly recall his pursuit of it and the exaltation he had felt upon finally being able to purchase it. Farrell would again break down in tears. Sobbing, sometimes clutching a whiskey, he would wander throughout the house till the wee hours of the morning, until the torment of self-pity was replaced by tipsy indifference. Returning to his study, he would fall asleep on the brown leather couch, forgetting that he would soon be separated from its kind embrace as well.

Such desperate suffering caused by separation from one's material possessions speaks volumes about our reliance upon the silent continuity of our environment. Each object that Farrell was separating from had its own specific meaning to him. The loss caused a rupture in their mutual biography, as if there had been an ongoing "dialogue" be‹ tween them that came to an abrupt halt with their parting of ways. Pain resulted from this. However, regardless of the specific meanings of this or that possession, the overall destabilization of the physi‹ cal surround that accompanies a divorce is invari‹ ably unsettling.

Familiar objects help us feel safe. They are con‹ tainers of our memory and anchors of our identity. We depend upon them to conduct our daily lives in their usual way. Our sense of safety is threat‹ ened when the environment around us changes in a dramatic manner. The psychological scaffold constituted by our material possessions is sud‹ denly shaken up and we feel cold and naked fear. But why does it take a loss to unmask how emo‹ tionally important our things were to us?

Ask those who have lost their possessions as a result of natural disasters as well as refugees who are fleeing political persecution. Loss of property in the wake of earthquakes, floods, and hurricanes can be astounding and so can its psychological im‹ pact. Countless newspaper columns, magazine articles, books, and films document such devasta‹ tion. However, they usually paint the picture with sweeping, broad strokes. Financial calculations, such as the $7 *billion* damage caused by Hurricane Hugo, which struck the Carolinas in 1989, are a staple of such reportage. What tends to get lost here is the personal anguish of specific people facing separation from specific things. The loss of a house, a car, furniture, and similar "big" things is of course hurtful. But the loss of "small" things can be equally distressing. A ruined stamp collection can cause lifelong suffering. A toolbox given by one's father that is now lost in a flood can be the source of sleepless nights for years. The emotional value of an object is in the proverbial eye of the beholder.

Immigrants and exiles are forever ready to acknowledge the significance of lost objects. While voluntary immigrants also suffer from having to part with familiar objects, the anguish of those who have had to leave their lands abruptly and not entirely of their choice is far greater, like the Jews of Eastern Europe fleeing Nazi persecution, the Hindus leaving parts of India during the country's bloody partition in 1947, the Palestinians whose lands have been taken over, and the Albanian and Kosovar Muslims facing the Serbian massacre of their communities.

Shalini Maitra, the daughter of an affluent landlord in Dhaka, became a refugee during the partition of India in 1947. Living in far less opulent surroundings in Calcutta, she continued to pine for her ancestral bungalow in her erstwhile homeland. Iman Hamadi, a Palestinian refugee living in Sudan, still gets teary when talking of the olive gardens in the lands lost to Israeli occupation. Numerous examples of this sort, unfortunately, can be given from all over the world.

The loss of land, home, nationality, and, above all, human dignity among these people is great. Interspersed in the larger picture are the details of losses that are small by comparison but no less heart-wrenching. A man's day-to-day physical possessions like clothes, wallet, shoes, and eyeglasses connect him to reality and society in an unassuming but deep manner. They afford him safety and social acceptability. Upon losing such objects, one feels strangely naked and robbed of human dignity. The saga of such losses is captured in the autobiographies, poems, fiction, and movies that are produced by the people thus affected. At other times, the sad eyes and sealed lips tell the stories that cannot otherwise be reported. And it sometimes takes a long time before such secret suffering becomes known.

This kind of traumatic loss of loved possessions can also happen in "civilian" circumstances. A striking example of this is when parents thoughtlessly discard their children's belongings.

Sarah Green, a fifty-two-year-old business manager, becomes teary-eyed anytime the mention of her childhood toys comes up during family reunions. Raised by a stern and caustic mother and a workaholic father, Sarah suffered intense neglect as a child. She has no memories of playing with her mother. Indeed, all she can recall from her childhood is chronic sarcasm from her mother and occasional spankings by her father. The rest is an abyss of loneliness and despair. Her only solace came from Erma, the maid, and her Barbie dolls ("dollies"), to which she was very attached. She also enjoyed riding her tricycle, which her grandfather had bought for her soon before his death. These meager supports were, however, lost when the family moved to another suburb. Sarah's mother not only fired the maid, she threw away Sarah's "dollies" and even her tricycle because it was too much trouble to pack them. Sarah withdrew inwardly, became more sad and forlorn. The pain persisted within her and was readily stirred up every time various family members got together and the topic of their move from one suburb to another came up.

Even more hurtful things are at times done to little children. One less recognized type of "child abuse," for instance, consists of asking children to give up their prized possessions.

Jim Reeves, a retired attorney in my neighborhood, told me of a soul-wrenching incidence of this sort from his childhood. He grew up with his lower-middle-class grandparents in rural Louisiana. His mother died when he was six years old and his father moved to Texas shortly afterward. Jim was left in the care of his grandparents. Off and on he would hear from his father. Sometimes he would receive a package containing a toy or a book. Jim clung to these tokens of affection from his largely absent father with all the psychological might he could muster. Once, when he was nine years old, he faced a horrible situation, one that in Leonard Shengold's words was tantamount to *soul murder*. He was invited to a schoolmate's birthday party but had nothing to take as a gift. His grandparents suggested that he give a book that he had recently received from his father. Otherwise, he would not be allowed to go since they were not about to buy something for him to take. Jim cried and cried but ultimately agreed to part with his father's gift to him. Something, however, broke within him that day. This happened some sixty years ago, but the hurt remains alive in Jim's heart today. To all appearances, he lives well: he has a big house, a reasonably happy family—and a large collection of rare books, although, to this day, he abhors lending them to others.

Such traumatic separations from one's loved possessions stand in sharp contrast to the reluctant parting with things on the part of a clutterer. The former involves having to give up highly cherished specific objects. The latter involves having to live with fewer things around one's self. The former is a passive experience, causing helplessness and pain. The latter, while anxiety producing, involves some participation on the part of the clutterer and even a halfhearted wish to be rid of a few things.

Decluttering

Americans are being suffocated by their things, yet the tendency to amass things has found its match in "the urge to purge." Jura Koncius of the *Washington Post*, who coined this phrase, calls the decluttering preoccupation the "new dieting" of today. As a result, a whole industry has cropped up to help people get rid of their extra "stuff."

According to the International Housewares Association, Americans spend more than $5 billion on space and closet organizers. Outlets such as Hold Everything, Organized Living, and the Container Store are doing enormous business promising to bring order to every nook and cranny of people's homes. A forceful nudge to get rid of useless things also comes from TV shows like *Clean Sweep* and *Mission: Organization,* as well as from magazines like *Real Simple,* which give you sage counsel on "When to Throw Things Out." Decluttering specialists offer all sorts of advice to people with homes that are overflowing with things. Peter Walsh, the dynamic organizer of *Clean Sweep,* tells you to "never keep more than three issues of one magazine." Don Aslett, who goes by the designation "America's #1 Cleaning Expert," recommends that you miniaturize your collections in order to enhance your livable space. Stephanie Culp, the author of *How to Conquer Clutter,* has even come up with "Ten Commandments to Reduce Clutter" (e.g., stop procrastinating and start cleaning now, give some things away, set limits upon what you acquire, and so on). There is also personalized professional help available. In addition to our personal therapists and personal trainers, we can now have our very own personal home organizers. The 2,200 members of the National Association of Professional Organizers are ready to help us throw away useless things that surround us so that we can lead a lean and clean life.

At the same time, the excesses of various decluttering gurus have made the living room of language itself quite cluttered. Thus we now have personality categories such as *stashers, spreaders, messies,* and *hoarders.* We have *clutter-bugs, clutter-traps,* and *clutter-busters.* There is a Messies Anonymous, headquartered in Florida. Even the designations of various types of clutter have caused their own lexical clutter. Thus we have *kiddie clutter, color clutter, mental clutter, virtual clutter* (resulting from the inability to erase e-mail messages), *atmospheric clutter, activity clutter,* and *relationship clutter,* among many others.

Surely the true pack rats among us could benefit from others pushing us to toss a few things away. The battle between the lust to acquire things and the pressure to discard them might be psychologically taxing but is certainly worth waging.

However, one has to first overcome the anxiety that the suggestion to declutter invariably causes. Nudged by someone to discard a few things, the clutter-prone individual feels tense and defensive, maybe even angry. And yet, if the pressure to declutter is continually and firmly applied, a willingness to part with some things gradually emerges. The clutterer might find the experience "not that bad after all." He might even start enjoying the throwing-away process and the relief and freedom that come from giving up adhesion to objects. Better-organized closets and more tidy living quarters reflect a rediscovered sense of personal autonomy, creating a sense of relief and joy.

Such positive aspects of "decluttering" lead some individuals to voluntarily reduce the material accompaniments of their lives. In still others, there develops a cyclical tendency to accumulate and discard things, which comes to resemble the well-known syndromes of bulimia and anorexia.

Letting go of things

Saying "good-bye" to things is integral to our lives. The three ways of parting with things discussed so far (losing them, being forcibly separated from them, and being cajoled to discard them) are only a subplot to this larger theme. At each stage of life, we leave a few things behind or give them away. We give up walkers when our own legs can fully support our weight. We outgrow cribs and move into "grown-up beds." We leave our tricycles for bicycles, which we replace with cars. The board games and toys that we enthusiastically played with at age ten or twelve are pushed to the background when we enter adolescence. As we grow and change, so do our things—the paraphernalia of identity. Every step of the way, life requires us to leave some of our possessions behind. That we do so with relative ease is because we do not really give up much. We replace one set of things with another that better fits our needs and wishes.

But parting with things takes on a new meaning during late middle age. Now we may begin to downsize and to plan the fate of our things after we are gone. Giving things away to those who are younger than us, especially our children and grand‹children, is a way to reduce the number of our pos‹sessions as well as ensure a legacy. Even so, it is difficult to say good‹bye to all we have amassed in our life. We feel reluctant to part with things that have had special meaning for us. Our pain is less‹ened if our loved ones understand our distress and offer us ways of renouncing our things that do not abruptly sever our ties to them.

While planning to move her elderly mother into an assisted‹living facility, Erin Nevin faced the task of disposing of the contents of her mother's house. The huge collection of books that was truly dear to her mother posed a problem. Sensing that her mother was not emotionally prepared to part with it, Erin came up with an innovative solution. She suggested that the books be donated to the library in the facility where her mother was going to live. Then she designed a beautiful label to be pasted on the inside cover of each book, saying that the book was a part of her mother's collection donated to the library. Erin's thoughtful gesture allowed her mother to let go of the books while maintaining an emotional tether to them.

In the end, we are what we possessed and what we leave behind. The things we leave behind might be cherished, embellished, disregarded, dreaded,

or hated. It all depends upon the lingering relation‑
ship between us (now as memories) and those who
are bereaved by our death, and upon the cultural
traditions in which our lives have unfolded. One
way or another, our things persist, living on after
we are dead. The great Argentinean poet Jorge
Luis Borges (1899–1986) makes a solemn state‑
ment to this effect in his poem titled "Things."

My cane, my pocket change, the rings of keys,
The obedient lock, the belated notes
The few days left to me will not find time
To read, the deck of cards, the tabletop,
A book, and crushed in its pages the withered
Violet, monument to an afternoon
Undoubtedly unforgettable, now forgotten,
The mirror in the west where a red sunrise
Blazes its illusion. How many things,
Files, doorsills, atlases, wine glasses, nails,
Serve us like slaves who never say a word,
Blind and so mysteriously reserved.
They will endure beyond our vanishing;
And they will never know that we have gone.

Although our things may literally outlast us, we
continue to live through (our) things. And it is
precisely here that an existential paradox winks at
us. We acquire permanence by no longer being

ourselves. At the beginning of life, we did not have the capacity to think of things as apart from us. At its end, we become a part of things and it is through them that we are remembered. Inter‹ twined with things in life, we become intermin‹ gled with them in death.

becoming a thing

Golders Green is the name of the place.

To get there, you take the London tube (Zone 3) to Golders Green station. As you exit the station, turn right onto Finchley Road and follow it under a bridge for a few blocks. After a leisurely five-minute walk, you will come across a quiet street called Hoope Lane. Turn right on it and within a minute or two you will find a beautifully maintained garden of several acres and in the middle of it the neo-Romanesque structure that is England's first crematorium. It is called Golders Green.

Inside the building, there is a room where glass cabinets are filled with neatly arranged urns and vases of varying shapes and sizes. These contain the ashes of some of the world's greatest luminaries.

As you slowly walk through the room, you read the names. Your heart begins to pound. T. S. Eliot, Alexander Fleming, Aldous Huxley, Vivian Leigh, Anna Pavlova, Peter Sellers, Bram Stoker, H. G. Wells, and, just when you think you have seen it all, Sigmund Freud. The encounter leaves you dumbfounded.

The emotions you feel are powerful and mixed. You are overwhelmed by awe and humility, which result from being in the presence of such talented people. You want to pay respect and homage to them. Then, mustering a bit of courage, you want to talk to them, show off your knowledge of their works, and thus establish familiarity with them. "I have read what you wrote and therefore have a sort of kinship with you." That's what you want to say to them. "I remember you, admire you, and hence I keep you alive." Paradoxically, this very thought reminds you that what you are faced with are not actual people but merely their ashes. Not human beings but things they have become. Fine, powdery gray dust with speckles of bone chips here and there. Inert, silent, and haplessly restricted to the inner contours of this or that particular vase. The awareness shakes you up. You realize that you have been carrying on a dialogue with inanimate objects. In effect, you have been talking to yourself. The whole experience now turns uncanny. Misty-eyed and slightly nervous, you leave the place. Nonetheless, some questions keep haunting you. Were these things once actual people? How could such great individuals have been reduced to ashes? Would all of us end up as things? If so, has the process already begun? Pushing the disturbing thoughts aside, you briskly walk back to the station and hop onto the subway. Your next stop is Madame Tussaud's.

A house of wax

The blurred boundary between what is alive and what is not and what are living and breathing human beings and what are mere things can indeed be disturbing. However, if this same overlap is presented to us in an aesthetically pleasing manner, the experience can be gratifying and playful. It might even add to the childlike joy of discovering the edge between reality and unreality. The renowned Madame Tussaud's Museum in London, where wax statues of great people from the past stand shoulder to shoulder with those of modern celebrities, is a case in point. Men, women, and children from all over the world throng to see its marvelous display of the lifelike figures of individuals as diverse as Winston Churchill and Tom Cruise, Mahatma Gandhi and Arnold Schwarzenegger, Isaac

Newton and Clint Eastwood, and Sigmund Freud and Margaret Thatcher. The museum—a "must-see" stop for the first-time tourist to London—was founded in 1835 by Marie Grosholz (1761–1850), a talented and determined Frenchwoman who later came to be known as Madame Tussaud.

Crafted with attention to the minutest details of their subjects, the museum's human approximations make one forget the distinction between animate and inanimate. Made of wax and attired in astutely appropriate costumes, they create the illusion of being fully alive. One almost expects them to begin walking and talking or, at least, to say hello and shake one's hand. It is amazing how this expected transformation of a thing into a human being is a matter of fun and games while the transformation of a human being into a thing, such as the one we are reminded of while visiting Golders Green, is sad and disturbing. Our reaction to seeing professional mimes in carnivals and amusement parks falls in between these extremes. By adopting a statuelike stillness and then suddenly showing movement ("coming alive"), these mimics of mortality impress upon us that the line between inanimate and animate is indeed thin. What appears to be a thing can turn out to be alive and, by implication, what is alive can turn into a thing. The former reassures us against our fears of mortality. The latter reminds us of our ultimate fate, death, and makes us nervous. We do not want to think about the time when we will cease to exist.

This is true despite the fact that all of us will sooner or later die and our bodies will be buried, cremated, or otherwise disposed of. We begin our lives, so to speak, as daydreams in our parents' minds and end them by becoming memories for our children and grandchildren; the latter is what Milan Kundera calls "immortality of a simple type." Interestingly, after our death it is our physical possessions (e.g., a wristwatch, a collection of books, our college diploma, some pieces of furniture) that assure that those left behind think of us from time to time. Our things become our posthumous publicity agents.

This much is known and congenial to most of us. Less recognized is the fact that not only do our things perpetuate our emotional presence beyond our actual life, but the thing we *become* after death (a corpse, ashes) is also of psychological use for others. After all, our dead bodies and our ashes are the recipient of strong emotions from those who cared about us when we were alive. Such emotions serve important functions for them. As living beings, we contributed to others' lives in one way. As "things," we do so in other ways. The transformation from a throbbing, pulsating, feeling, and thinking being to an inanimate thing, however useful that might turn out to be, is hard to fathom. The fact is that, in small doses, it is happening on an everyday basis. While, as an overall organism, we continue to live, parts of us keep dying.

The hair on my barber's floor

The imperceptible yet ongoing decay of the human body as it passes through time is an illustration of how the animate gradually turns into the inanimate. Even the waste products that come out of our bodies every so often demonstrate that what is one minute an integral part of a living being can become merely a thing the next minute. What brought this home to me most sharply was a glance at the hair scattered on my barber Tony's floor.

One day while I was getting a haircut, my eyes went to the clumps of the previous customer's hair on the floor. And once Tony began cutting my hair, I could see similar samples of my own—now quite gray—hair on the floor. The sight made me ask whether the hair that had been cut from my head still belonged to me. It somehow did not seem to, yet to say that I did not feel any affinity or sense of ownership toward it would also be a lie. More significantly, I became aware that, due to the decisive intervention of a pair of scissors, what was a part of me moments ago had become an inanimate thing, cold and, frankly, a bit distasteful to behold. Now, let me hasten to add that Tony is a gentle and kind man. His purpose in cutting my hair is to improve my appearance, make me feel comfortable, and sustain my social acceptability. From his perspec‹ tive, it is all a benign act. The follicular massacre that occurs daily in his shop is merely collateral damage as far as Tony is concerned. I, however, am left a little unnerved. If a part of me can so readily turn into a thing, what assurance is there that the whole of me would not succumb to the seduction of eternal inertia? Thoughts of death begin to sur‹ face in my mind. They make me uneasy. Tony and I exchange a few polite remarks. I pay the bill and leave. Looking back, I can see that parts of me are still lying on Tony's floor.

Beyond burial and cremation

In contrast to such transformations of the parts of a living organism is its total and ultimate transition into the realm of non‹living. Death, the end point of life, inevitably arrives and changes us from feel‹ ing, thinking, and dreaming individuals with hopes

and aspirations into dead bodies—cadavers—
which are then disposed of in all sorts of ways.
These vary with each particular culture and era.

The two most common fates of our dead bodies—the thing we become—are burial and cremation. The former has long been the mainstream
way of disposing of dead bodies in Judeo-Christian
and Islamic cultures, although the latter is becoming more popular in contemporary Western soci-
eties. Burial creates the illusion that we still have a
home on this earth. Our graves are called our "resting places," suggesting our beds. The idea of having
a grave is somehow soothing; it makes us feel as if
we would rest a little, then get up again and go
about our business. In imagining our graves, we in-
dulge in a bit of a Rip Van Winkle fantasy, it seems.
No wonder burial is still the most common way of
disposing of our bodies after death.

Cremation, on the other hand, affords us a different sort of illusory omnipotence. We can put
our ashes in cute little boxes, like those of Godiva
chocolates, and distribute one to each of our dear
ones. Besides, getting cremated saves us a hell of a
lot of money; it is far cheaper than being buried.
These two reasons, being able to be at various
places simultaneously and saving money, seem to
be responsible for the increasing popularity of cre-

mation in the West. Families that are geographically separated as a result of divorce or migration especially prefer this way of disposing of dead bodies. If one is cremated, one can be close to one's parents and children both, after death, even if they live in different cities or countries. Each party can have some of the ashes. No need for the bereaved to travel long distances to visit a grave. No torment for the dying to choose where to be buried.

Burial, in any case, is no simple matter. It involves all sorts of steps and rituals. Moreover, there is a vast array of accoutrements (e.g., caskets, hearses, embalming machines) associated with burying the dead, as becomes unmistakably evident upon a visit to the National Museum of Funeral History in Houston, Texas. There are considerable variations in the manner of burial. For instance, Christians and Jews have their bodies placed in caskets before being buried, while most Muslims have theirs simply wrapped in a sheet of cloth. All three groups bury their dead supine. However, this too is not ubiquitous. The ancient Chinese had a tradition of burying their dead in an erect, standing posture, and the Lingayat Brahmans of India bury corpses in a Samadhi, a cross-legged sitting posture.

Standing, sitting, or lying down, the fact is the saga of our corpses does not end with their burial.

Soon our new homes, our graves, acquire a life of their own. Snug in our underground resting places, we can see the fuss our loved ones make over the size, shape, and style of our epitaphs and gravestones. Our names are chiseled in marble or granite and our dates of birth and death are dutifully inscribed. If we get lucky, an apt phrase summarizing our life or a poem comes to adorn our gravestones as well. And, by God, we continue to exert all sorts of influence upon those we have left behind. They come to visit our graves and feel guilty if they do not do so. When they do come, they bring us flowers as if we can still see and smell them. They talk to us and, believe it or not, even seek our forgiveness for their misdeeds and our blessings for their future undertakings, especially marriage. Sometimes they bring their children— born after our death—and their potential spouses for a sort of "introduction" with us.

Consider the various ways in which we can contribute to society as dead bodies. Mary Roach, the author of *Stiff: The Curious Lives of Human Cadavers,* deals extensively with this matter. A condensed version of her list includes the following:

- Our dead bodies are used by medical students to learn human anatomy and by future surgeons to practice their operating skills.

- As cadavers, some of us are used in laboratory experiments testing automobile safety during crashes and accidents.

- Our posthumous generosity lets others have our organs and can give an additional lease to others' lives after our own term has expired.

- In a similar vein, though admittedly on a much less frequent basis, our body parts can be used for medicinal purposes. Placenta, for instance, is still occasionally consumed by women to ward off postpartum depression. Lest you regard this as entirely esoteric, Roach is there to remind you that the popular cooking show *TV Dinners* on British television recently aired a garlic-fried placenta segment!

Some bizarre fates of our dead bodies

Our dead bodies can also undergo macabre violations by sexual perverts ("necrophiliacs"), who extract lascivious gratification from us when we are totally unable to thwart their intrusions. Utterly helpless, we submit to their deviant impulse, hoping it to be a onetime occurrence and praying that the act brings a modicum of peace to our violator's tormented soul. Lest such practices be dismissed as unimaginable, let us be reminded of the horrible violations of human bodies committed by the Nazis during the Holocaust. Lamp shades and purses made out of Jewish inmates' skin give testimony to the depth human beings can sink to in their maltreatment of dead bodies.

Serial killers sometimes desecrate the corpse and its parts in this way. Jeffrey Dahmer cannibalized human organs, cut parts from the body, and kept them in his refrigerator for storage. Others are known to enucleate eyes, cut out tongues, and decapitate human bodies in the dark surge of hostile omnipotence. But one does not have to be depraved to commit such acts.

Under exceptional circumstances, such as the combat of war, all of us are vulnerable to regress and lose our usual civility and moral restraint. Primitive, animal-like callousness can then emerge and lead to shocking acts of dehumanization and violence. The following incident, reported to me by Bobby Sasso, a Vietnam veteran, demonstrates this point:

> Once I was standing knee deep in a marsh in Vietnam, gun in my hand, eyes and ears alert for any sign of approaching enemy. I was not alone. There were five of us, each looking, watching for the same danger, all five advancing with slow, measured steps.

Suddenly this guy, a nice kid from Minnesota, whose name I am having difficulty recalling, came up to me and asked, "Do you like figs?" Puzzled by his question given the circumstances we were in, I responded by saying that I could take them or leave them. Upon this, he offered me a brown paper bag, opening it slightly and saying, "Here, try one." Absentmindedly, I put my hand in the bag to pull one out. I thought, What the hell, I will try one. But as soon as I got one out, I was horrified to note that the "fig" was actually a human ear. More shocking was the fact that the bag was full of human ears. He, on the other hand, found my reaction hilarious and laughed uncontrollably. Found the whole situation funny. He told me that he had cut these ears off from the dead bodies of Vietnamese soldiers and was planning to take his collection back to the USA as a wartime souvenir. The guy found nothing odd in what he was saying or doing. In fact, he found my squeamishness to be silly.

Away from such tragic extremes of human behavior during war but still bizarre are the outlandish ways in which the mavericks among us decide the fate of their own corpses. Note the following examples.

- The body of Ted Williams (1918–2002), the renowned Boston Red Sox player, was cryonically preserved by the Alcor Life Extension Foundation in Scottsdale, Arizona, at the behest of his son, John Henry Williams. It was John's idea that his father's body could be kept frozen for a long time so that his DNA could one day be used to clone him.

- Timothy Leary (1920–1996), the 1960s flower child turned psychedelic drug-taking spiritual guru, had his ashes shot into space. After cremation, about seven grams of Leary's ashes were taken and placed in a nine-by-twelve-inch canister, which also had similar amounts of ashes of *Star Trek* creator Gene Roddenberry, space physicist Gerrard O'Neill, and rocket scientist Krafft Ehricke. A rocket propelled the capsule three hundred miles above the Earth, where it was expected to orbit from about eighteen months to ten years and then burn up in the atmosphere. "It will be like a shooting star," said Charles Chafer, co-owner of Celestis, the company that arranged the blastoff.

- The inventor of the Frisbee, Ed Headrick (1924–2002), instructed his family that once he passed away, he should be cremated and his ashes incorporated into discs so that he could fly like Frisbees. Ed's family respected his wishes, and with the help of Discraft, a Frisbee manufacturing company, created two Ed Memorial Discs, which are Frisbees containing his ashes. The announcement of this product included the following statement: "We understand that some people may not want to play with the discs and they might end up on a wall as collectibles. Therefore, we are selling the discs as sets of two so that you can at least play with one and keep the other in a pristine state." The set of Frisbees costs $210, including shipping and handling. All proceeds go to the non-profit "Steady" Ed Memorial Museum.

Capitalizing on this characteristically American allure of individualism beyond death, many business enterprises offering novel alternatives to burial or cremation have cropped up. Life Gem Company of suburban Chicago is offering to make diamonds out of the carbon found in cremated bones, and Eternal Reefs of Atlanta is mixing human remains and concrete to make coastal reefs. Working in close collaboration with selected funeral homes across the nation, the Chicago outfit creates diamonds by heating the mortal remains to extreme temperatures and then putting pressure on the carbon. Its services can cost anywhere from two to thirteen thousand dollars, and the diamonds it produces can have great variability of size and shape. Not one to be left behind, the Atlanta company has offered to create a memorial for the World Trade Center terrorist attack victims by building an offshore reef to attract and shelter marine life.

On a day-to-day basis, the firm mixes cremated remains with cement to create large reef balls, which are dropped to the ocean floor to help rebuild deteriorating natural reefs or create new ones. This particular way of "becoming one with the universe" is the preferred mode for those who want to be buried at sea but whose relatives find it too cumbersome to dispose of the entire body in the ocean. And, as one might expect, friends and relatives of the deceased often return for scuba diving at the memorial reef sites.

Are such "extensions" of life likely to remind us that our being alive is but a short pause between the transition from being our parents' fantasy to being our offspring's memory? Or, in their grotesque denial of our end, would such practices stunt the normal and health-promoting process of grief and mourning? The most likely answer to these questions lies in the fact that these practices involve such a minuscule proportion of the population that they are unlikely to have any significant impact on the overall view we have of death and the disposal of the dead. They most likely represent passing trends whose novelty would be difficult to sustain after a while. The more important thing to consider here is how the boundaries between man and thing can become blurred. Sometimes this blurring hap-

pens in actuality and at other times the dehuman‹
ization of a human being is only on a metaphorical
level.

Was Mohammad Atta a machine?

Imagine for a moment that you are Mohammad
Atta, the ringleader of the September 11th terror‹
ists who rammed planes into the World Trade Cen‹
ter and the Pentagon. You walk up to the check‹in
counter, show your ticket, and ask for an aisle seat.
All this time you know what you are up to, but you
keep it to yourself and appear entirely composed.
You get your boarding pass, thank the check‹in
agent, and walk toward the security clearance. You
are fully aware that your intention is to kill thou‹
sands of people within half an hour or so. You also
know that you, yourself, are going to die along with
them. Yet you appear peaceful and walk onto the
plane like any other person. You take your seat,
buckle the security belt, say hello to the person sit‹
ting next to you, and leisurely leaf through the in‹
flight magazine. The plane takes off. You look
around. There is a bald man in the row to your left.
A blond woman who has a bandage on her wrist.
Two boys of eight and ten talking loudly to each

other. An elderly woman who is already fast asleep. And there are so many others. You know that you are going to kill all of them in a matter of minutes, yet you remain calm. You also know that the fireball that the plane is soon to become will engulf your body as well, burning and charring it beyond recognition. But somehow the awareness does not bother you. Or perhaps you no longer register such "minor inconveniences." You have a job to do and that is all there is to it. No empathy for anybody. No concern for yourself. No recognition that someone's husband or wife or son or daughter or mother or father might be waiting for him or her to arrive. No wish and no dream for your own future. No thoughts of your parents, siblings, and children. The work has to be done. Everybody has to be killed, including yourself. You do not care about anything else. You are a walking machine, a human bomb. In fact, you are not human at all.

I know that you would have difficulty putting yourself in the scenario described above. You would be unable to become so utterly indifferent to the lives of others and certainly of yourself. You would be scared, full of anticipatory remorse, and therefore incapable of the callousness of a terrorist. I know. I have tried this mental exercise and failed miserably. I just couldn't imagine killing people nor could I envision facing a violent death myself with equanimity. You and I are simply too human; we care about ourselves and about others. Mr. Atta, I presume, had become a machine.

But how does this happen? What leads someone to lose the essence of his humanity? And what is humanity after all? The answer to this last question is that "humanity" is what aligns us with our fellow human beings in a most fundamental way. "Humanity" consists of the sharing of similar physiognomy and anatomy, common needs for identity and self-expression, capacity for thought and thinking, acquisition of language, barriers against murder and incest, group affiliation, and elaboration of myths and rituals. The terrorist becomes devoid of this human core and therefore can evacuate all concern for himself and others. His dehumanization is largely a matter of Janus-faced strategy. In the external reality, killing innocent bystanders (in order to influence their political rulers) is made easy for him by viewing them as mere pawns in the game. In the internal world, dehumanizing others protects him from the dread of empathy (which would preclude his actions) and the emergence of remorse (which would prevent his repeating such actions). Dehumanization of his own self, spurred by the adrenaline-pumping exhortations of religious or political variety, is also essentially strategic. A self that has been transformed into a machine has greater immunity against fears of bodily harm and less sadness over a wasted life. It is useful as a weapon.

A further paradox. When we are turned into a thing physically by our death, we can stay useful to others (e.g., as cadavers we can be used for teaching anatomy and for automobile crash tests), but when we are turned only mentally into a thing, we can be dangerous to both ourselves and others. Physical death is integral to the "order of things" and therefore carries a certain kind of dignity. Mental death is the result of humiliation and abuse and intends to clone the trauma by making others suffer.

After "the end"

The Great Transition from animate to inanimate that awaits all of us is called death. Talking of burials, cremations, and all sorts of other curious ways of disposing of dead bodies has served as a deceptive cloak of lexical embroidery to the hard and, if you will, cold fact that in the long run, we all die and end up as "things." Inanimate, immobile, mute, without sentiment, thought, or volition. I could go on and on, but the celebrated phrase "from ashes to ashes and dust to dust" captures it all.

And once we die, our bodies—the "thing" aspect of ourselves—become part of this universe in

one way or the other. Our blood assumes the stillness of this earth and our bones fall apart like an
orphan's toy. Our flesh rots. Our ashes are dis-
persed and our bodies are eaten up by underground insects and microbes. Bit by bit, the
distinction between what we were as human beings—with love, hate, malice, lust, envy, and joy—
and what a piece of earth is or a worm crawling out
of a small pocket of soil is or a flower opening its
petals for the first time is becomes unclear. The
water from our bodies is absorbed by the land, if
we are buried, and is evaporated into the air, if we
are cremated. Either way, the water from our bodies adds to the bodies of water in this universe, and
from them we rise as clouds and then fall on the
ground as raindrops. Sometimes, if we are truly
lucky, it is our grandchild or great-grandchild or
even great-great-grandchild who catches the rain-
drop that we have become in her little hand and
protects us from hitting the ground too hard. In
that brief and shining moment of human kindness,
the tears of those who cried the day we passed away
are transformed into a wet inscription of joy on the
child's palm. We live, we die, and we live again. In
the process, we keep changing shape. One moment
of history sees us as a living being, the next as a
thing, and when everything is said and done, it
turns out to have been the same anyway.

epilogue: a little silver box inside the parrot's heart

Glorious kingdoms, daring bandits, shy brides, amputated hands, trees that kept family secrets, and animals that spoke in human tongues—all appeared at one time or another in the bedtime stories my grandmother told me. She never stuck to a set plot. She kept changing it, making the story shorter or longer depending upon her mood, deftly mixing the elements of one story with those of another, as I grew sleepier and sleepier.

One character in these stories was the king who was immune to all physical assaults and injuries. Indeed, it was nearly impossible to kill him. The reason for this was simple. He had taken his soul out of his body and put it in a little silver box. Then he ordered that a parrot be brought to him. Carefully he incised the chest of this parrot, placed the silver box inside the parrot's heart, and released the bird to fly over the jungles nearby his kingdom. With his soul tucked inside the parrot, the king was safe from attack. All attempts at assassinating him failed. Smart? Well, at least that is what my grandmother and I thought.

Time passed. My grandmother died. I grew up, became a man, then a father. The impervious king was put on a shelf in the dusty cupboard of childhood amnesia. Then one day I was reminded of him with sudden and sharp clarity. While introducing my daughter to a group of colleagues, I found myself recounting the story of this king. Beaming with fatherly pride, I pointed to my daughter and said that she was my parrot.

Later that evening, I wondered about the meanings of this parable. I surmised that it showed that one can truly be harmed only if one's loved ones are put in jeopardy. After all, the king would have died if someone captured and killed the parrot. However, with the passage of time, I began to see a deeper message here, and that is if we actively love others—put our souls in them, so to speak—then we become stronger and can bear life's hardships without wincing.

Satisfied with these two layers of understanding, I reshelved the image of this king in the back corners of my mind. Forgot all about him. Till I began writing this book. Now an element that I had not noted in this story caught my attention. I realized that in focusing upon the king and the parrot, I had overlooked the silver box. A profound implication of the story dawned upon me. In establishing a smooth confluence between man (the king), animal (the parrot), and thing (the silver box), the Indian folktale declared that in the eyes of nature, they are all the same. Sometimes they stand in opposition and appear separate. At other times, they symbolize one another or even merge into one another. We ourselves, who at first do not know these distinctions, go about acquiring so many things, only to leave them behind and become ourselves a thing in the end. Ashes to ashes, dust to dust. The king had the wisdom to exploit this seamlessness in nature for the purpose of his defense. He was indeed smart. And so was my grandmother.

notes

CHAPTER 1: acquiring and using things

page 18 This excerpt is taken from Pablo Neruda's poem "Ode to Things," which appears in his book *Odes to Common Things* (Boston: Bulfinch Press, 1994).

page 19 "We constantly discover, or as Freud would..." Sigmund Freud first spoke of "object choice" in his "Three Essays on the Theory of Sexuality" (1905) in *The Complete Psychological Works of Sigmund Freud* (London: Hogarth Press, 1953), 7: 125–243. He noted that adult choices of "objects" (which in his vocabulary stood for human beings) were actually based upon early-childhood prototypes of the same. This gave rise to the idea that one never really "discovers" an "object" but merely "rediscovers" it. I have extended this notion of Freud to man's relationship with physical objects here. In essence, I am suggesting that the physical objects we find in adult life to be gratifying often contain shades and textures of those from our childhood. This past-to-present link in the selection of physical objects is most marked in the case of immigrants, as will be shown in the chapter "Nostalgic Things."

page 20 "As *naked apes*, which is what the ethologist . . ." Desmond Morris, *The Naked Ape* (New York: Random House, 1967).

page 21 "As a result, the world is full of useful things . . ." *Jorge Luis Borges: Selected Poems*, ed. Alexander Coleman (New York: Viking Press, 1999).

page 22 "Donald Winnicott, the British pediatrician turned psychoanalyst, emphasizes . . ." For further explication of these ideas, see Donald Winnicott, "Transitional Objects and Transitional Phenomena: A Study of the First Not-Me Possession," *International Journal of Psychoanalysis* 34 (1953): 89–97.

page 23 "The fact that potential groundwork for . . ." J. Huxley, *Essays of a Biologist* (London: Chatto and Windus, 1926).

CHAPTER 2: collecting and hoarding things

page 29 "Terry Kovel, who writes the *Kovels' Antiques . . .*" *Kovels' Antiques and Collectibles* (New York: Three Rivers Press, 2002).

page 34 "Lesser-known individuals have also amassed . . ." The list of unusual collections following this sentence is taken from the *Guinness Book of World Records*, ed. Claire Folkard (New York: Bantam Books, 2004).

page 38 "Bottle caps are okay, navel fluff is not." Those who find it hard to believe that people collect navel fluff would find "The Incredible World of Navel Fluff" on www.feargod. net both amusing and informative.

page 47 "Inability to discard anything, buying excessive quantites . . ." The practice of picking up things from other people's trash has been elevated to an art by the residents of Manhattan. Their apartments are frequently furnished and decorated with curbside items discarded by others. Ted Botha provides a fascinating account of this in his book *Mongo* (New York: Bloomsbury, 2004).

page 47 "Franz Lidz of the *New York Times* gives the following . . ." This information appears in the article "The Paper Chase" by Franz Lidz, the *New York Times,* October 26, 2003, sec. 14, p. 1.

page 48 "None of these tales, however, comes close to . . ." For more details on the Collyer brothers, see Franz Lidz's book *Ghosty Men: The Strange but True Story of the Collyer Brothers, New York's Greatest Hoarders* (New York: Bloomsbury, 2003).

CHAPTER 3: nostalgic things

page 57 "At the heart of nostalgia . . ." The renowned Viennese psychoanalyst Edith Sterba was the first to offer an in-depth psychological study of nostalgia in her paper "Homesickness and Maternal Breast," *Psychiatric Quarterly* 14 (1940): 701–707. Prominent among the more recent contributions to this topic are David Werman's article "Normal and Pathological Nostalgia," *Journal of the American Psychoanalytic Association* 25 (1977): 387–398, and Leslie Sohn's paper "Nostalgia," *International Journal of Psychoanalysis* 64 (1983): 203–211.

page 57 "This sense of loss, and yet of gain . . ." It was Freud who first pointed out that we have a tendency to overidealize people, things, and places that we have lost. This notion appears in his 1917 paper "Mourning and Melancholia" in *The Complete Psychological Works of Sigmund Freud* (London: Hogarth Press, 1955), 14: 239–258.

page 58 "We—all of us—go to cocktail parties . . ." This passage appears in Wheelis's book *The Illusionless Man* (New York: Colophon Books/Harper & Row, 1966), pp. 148–149.

page 60 "Oftentimes the main trauma of immigration . . ." Further elaboration on this matter appears in Stanley Denford's article "Going Away," *International Journal of Psychoanalysis* 59 (1981): 325–332.

page 61 "Throughout his life, de Chirico . . ." This point has been made most emphatically by de Chirico's biographer, James Sobysee, in his book *Giorgio de Chirico* (New York: The Museum of Modern Art, 1958).

page 62 "The immigrant's home becomes a refuge . . ." In my book *Immigration and Identity: Turmoil, Treatment, and Transformation* (Northvale, N.J.: Jason Aronson, 1999), I have elucidated the multifaceted measures that an immigrant undertakes in order to bolster his internally destabilized identity.

page 62 "Having had to leave against his will . . ." "Protective rites of farewell" is a phrase coined by Leon and Rebecca Grinberg to underscore that the opportunity of saying goodbye to loved people and places lessens the trauma of leaving. It appears in their coauthored book, *Psychoanalytic Perspectives on Immigration and Exile* (New Haven, Conn: Yale University Press, 1989).

page 64   Marcel Proust, *Remembrance of Things Past,* vol. 2 (New York: Random House, 1934).

page 66   Judith Guest, *Ordinary People* (New York: Ballantine Books, 1976).

page 66   Anne Tyler, *The Accidental Tourist* (New York: Alfred A. Knopf, 1985).

page 67   "The possessions in the third category . . ." The term "linking objects" has been coined by the psychoanalyst Vamik Volkan and appears in a number of his publications. The most important and comprehensive among these is his book *Linking Objects and Linking Phenomena: A Study of the Forms, Symptoms, Metapsychology, and Therapy of Complicated Mourning* (New York: International Universities Press, 1981).

page 68   Vamik Volkan and Elizabeth Zintel, *Life After Loss: The Lessons of Grief* (New York: Scribner, 1993).

page 69   "Is the power attributed to old objects . . ." Daniel Geahchan, "Deuli et nostalgie," *Revue française de Psychanalyse* 32 (1968): 39–65.

page 70   "A highly private man who published . . ." For details of Wallace Nutting's photographic career, see Michael Ivankovich's *The Collector's Guide to Wallace Nutting Pictures: Identification and Pricing* (Paducah, Ky.: Collectors Books, 1997). Nutting himself wrote a number of books. Most of these are about Windsor furniture, American antique clocks, and Colonial utensils and hardware. He also wrote a detailed volume about his life under the curiously unimaginative title *Wallace Nutting's Biography* (Framingham, Mass.: Old America Books, 1936).

CHAPTER 4: sacred things

page 78 "The anguished response of the North American Hindu community . . ." The bathroom fixture company that produced a series of "Sacred Seats," including one depicting the Hindu deity Ganesha, is called "Sittin' Pretty." The seats were withdrawn from the market in response to protests from the North American Hindu community.

page 78 "More familiar is the uproar created by New York Catholics . . ." The Mapplethorpe Censorship Controversy: Chronology of Events, www.publiceye.org.

page 83 "This line of thinking finds support from . . ." These definitions are taken from *Webster's Ninth New Collegiate Dictionary* (Springfield, Mass.: Merriam-Webster Inc., 1983), pp. 939–1035.

page 87 Salman Rushdie, *Satanic Verses* (New York: Viking, 1988).

CHAPTER 5: sexy things

page 94 "In other words, what Freud had described . . ." For Sigmund Freud's description of the Oedipus complex and its impact on the choices we make in our romantic and sexual lives, see the following two of his papers: "A Special Type of Object Choice Made by Men" (1910) in *The Complete Psychological Works of Sigmund Freud* (London: Hogarth Press, 1957), 11: 163–175, and "On the Universal Tendency to Debasement in the Sphere of Love" (1912) in *The Complete Psychological Works of Sigmund Freud* (London: Hogarth Press, 1957), 11: 178–190.

page 96 "Indeed, in a 1990 study conducted in . . ." D. M. Buss, "Sex Differences in Human Mate Preferences: Evolutionary Hypotheses Tested in 37 Cultures," *Behavioral and Brain Sciences* 12 (1989): 1–14.

page 97 "Almost ten million American adults read . . ." This is according to Playboy Enterprises, Inc., whose Web site can be accessed at www.playboyenterprises.com.

page 97 "All in all, pornography is an . . ." *Report of the U.S. Commission on Obscenity and Pornography* (1970), quoted in D. Symons, *The Evolution of Human Sexuality* (New York: Oxford University Press, 1979), p. 171.

page 98 "Robert Stoller, who investigated the psychology of . . ." For Stoller's theoretically sound and eminently readable views on the nature of sexual perversion, see his book *Perversion: The Erotic Form of Hatred* (New York: Pantheon Books, 1975).

page 99 "Freud declared that 'we never regard . . .'" Sigmund Freud, "Three Essays on the Theory of Sexuality" (1905) in *The Complete Psychological Works of Sigmund Freud* (London: Hogarth Press, 1953), 7: 135–243.

page 99 "Ariel Arango, a psychoanalyst practicing in Argentina . . ." This passage appears on page 125 of Ariel Arango's book *Dirty Words: Psychoanalytic Insights* (Northvale, N.J.: Jason Aronson, 1989).

page 100 "What Freud had said about the nature of . . ." Sigmund Freud, "Fetishism" (1927) in *The Complete Psychological Works of Sigmund Freud* (London: Hogarth Press, 1961), 11: 152–157.

page 103 "A study by the social anthropologist . . ." J. M. Townsend, "Mate Selection Criteria: a Pilot Study," *Ethology and Sociobiology* 10 (1989): 241–253.

page 104 Charles Darwin, *The Origin of Species* (London: John Murray, 1859).

page 105 Nancy Etcoff, *The Survival of the Prettiest* (New York: Anchor Books, 1999).

page 106 "According to the evolutionary scientists of beauty . . ." For Richard Dawkins's views on the determinates of physical beauty, see his books *The Blind Watchmaker* (New York: W. W. Norton, 1987) and *River Out of Eden* (New York: Basic Books, 1995).

page 108 "And if such arguments appear incredible . . ." For this and other provocative ideas of Desmond Morris, see his book *The Naked Ape* (New York: McGraw-Hill, 1967).

page 112 "Take a look at the list of foreign objects . . ." D. B. Busch and J. R. Starling, "Rectal Foreign Bodies: Case Reports and a Comprehensive Review of the World's Literature," *Surgery* 3 (1986): 512–519.

CHAPTER 6: hybrid things

page 118 For a proper dictionary definition of the word *hybrid*, see *Webster's Ninth New Collegiate Dictionary* (Springfield, Mass.: Merriam-Webster, Inc., 1983), p. 589.

page 119 A recent exhibition organized by the Walker Arts Center . . ." The details of *Strangely Familiar: Design and Everyday Life*, an exhibition organized by the Walker Arts Center,

Minneapolis, can be found on its November/December 2003 Web site. To access it, go to www.carnegiemuseums.org.

page 122 "A more dramatic illustration of multiformal . . ." For details on Di Bitonto's "Mutant Vase," see www.benzadesign.com.

page 122 "An example is constituted by the . . ." For details on Pellone's "Hello Coaster for Two," see www.benzadesign.com.

page 123 "A less festive example is the highly unusual . . ." Mention of the New Zealand woman's enterprise and other cremation urns of unusual nature is to be found in David Kelly's article "Vessels of Change: As Cremation Numbers Rise, Urns Add a Dash of Individuality," the *Philadelphia Inquirer,* November 29, 2002, p. D·1.

page 124 For further details on man·animal conflation in Greek mythology, see *Bullfinch's Mythology: The Greek and Roman Fables Illustrated,* complied by Bryan Holme (New York: Viking Press, 1979).

page 128 "An example is Kaboom . . ." Sam Lubell's article "Suicide Bomber Game Tests the Boundaries of Taste" in the *New York Times,* December 5, 2002, p. G·9, discusses the controversy surrounding Kaboom: The Suicide Bomber Game in some detail, noting that the game had been played more than 875,000 times and www.NewGrounds.com, the site on which the game had been released, contained hundreds of approving reviews.

page 128 "Not motivated by such greed and certainly . . ." There are a large number of books and Web sites on M. C. Escher's work. A collection of essays about Escher and his work, including one by the artist himself, is the edited volume *The World of M. C. Escher* by J. L. Locher (New York: Harry N. Abrams, 1972).

page 129 "Billy Collins, a former Poet Laureate . . ." The excerpt is taken from the poem "Creatures," which appears in Collins's latest collection, *Nine Horses* (New York: Random House, 2002), pp. 49–50.

CHAPTER 7: fake things

page 142 "In the spring of 2002, archaeologists, theologians . . ." Aaron Davis has covered this entire affair in his article "Experts Say Burial Box Mentioning Jesus Is a Forgery," appearing in the *Philadelphia Inquirer,* June 19, 2003, p. A.2.

page 142 "The French scholar Andre Lamaire . . ." Lamaire's article on James's ossuary appeared in *Biblical Archeology Review* 121 (2002): 1–17.

page 145 "Two outstanding art forgers who made . . ." For a listing of the twentieth century's most notorious forgers, including Hans van Meegeren and Tom Keating, go to www.musuemofhoaxes.com and look for "Index Hoaxorum: 1900–1998."

page 145 "Bruce Gimelson, who is a dealer and . . ." Gimelson's quote is taken from *Business Week* On-Line, April 3, 2000, P.2. To access it, go to www.businessweek.com/2000/00. Bruce Gimelson has an extensive Web site of his own, www.gimelson.com, which deals with art, antique, and autograph cost appraisals as well as detection of forgeries.

page 148 For details on Joseph Cosey's life, see the Web site of Courtroom Television Network. Its address is www.crimelibrary.com.

CHAPTER 8: misplacing, losing, and letting go of things

page 160 "We might attribute our loss to 'carelessness' without realizing . . ." For reasons underlying such "mistakes," see Sigmund Freud's "The Psychopathology of Everyday Life" (1901) in *The Complete Works of Sigmund Freud* (London: Hogarth Press, 1960), 6: 1–279.

page 164 The loss caused a rupture in their mutual . . ." The idea that things might have their own "biography" is the brainchild of Igor Kopytoff. He suggests that in viewing anything we might raise the following questions: Where does the thing come from? Who made it? What has been its history so far and what would one consider to be an ideal career for it? To quote Kopytoff, "To us, a biography of a painting by Renoir that ends up in an incinerator is as tragic, in its way, as the biography of a person who ends up murdered." For more of his views, see Igor Kopytoff, "The Cultural Biography of Things: Commoditization as Process" in *The Social Life of Things: Commodities in Cultural Perspective,* ed. Arjun Appadurai (Cambridge, U.K.: Cambridge University Press, 1986), pp. 64–91.

page 165 "Financial calculations, such as the $7 *billion* damage . . ." For the monetary and emotional havoc caused by hurricanes in the Carolinas, see Jay Barnes's *North Carolina's Hurricane History,* 3rd ed. (Chapel Hill, N.C.: University of North Carolina Press, 2001).

page 166 "Immigrants and exiles are forever ready to . . ." For further details on the experience of nostalgia in immigrants and exiles, see my book *Immigration and Identity: Turmoil, Treatment, and Transformation* (Northvale, N.J.: Jason Aronson, 1999).

page 169   "Once, when he was nine years old . . ." The concept of "soul murder" is described in Leonard Shengold's *Soul Murder: The Effects of Childhood Abuse and Deprivation* (New Haven, Conn.: Yale University Press, 1989).

page 170   "Americans are being suffocated by . . ." This information is taken from Jura Koncius's article "Clutter Control: Helping Us Find Places for Our Stuff Has Become a Booming Business," the *Times-Picayune*, March 14, 2004, pp. E-1–2.

page 170   "According to the International Housewares Association . . ." Ibid.

page 171   "Don Aslett, who goes by the designation . . ." See Don Aslett, *Clutter's Last Stand: It's Time to De-Junk Your Life* (Cincinnati, Ohio: Writer's Digest Books, 1984).

page 171   "Stephanie Culp, the author of . . ." See Stephanie Culp, *How to Conquer Clutter* (Cincinnati, Ohio: Writer's Digest Books, 1989).

page 171   "The 2,200 members of the . . ." The membership of this group has grown from five people when it was founded in 1985 to 2,200 in 2004. The full-time organizers who are its members can make from $40,000 to $200,000 a year. For further details regarding this group, go to www.napo.net.

page 175   Borges's poem "Things" has been taken from *Jorge Luis Borges: Selected Poems*, ed. Alexander Coleman (New York: Viking Press, 1999) p. 277.

CHAPTER 9: becoming a thing

page 180   For biographical details on Marie Grosholz ("Madame Tussaud"), see *Madam Tussaud and the History of Waxworks* by Pamela Pilbeam (London: Hambledon and London, 2003).

page 185   "Moreover, there is a vast array of . . ." For a glimpse of various types of caskets, embalming machines, hearses, and other funeral-related accoutrements, visit www.nmfh.org.

page 186   Mary Roach, *Stiff: The Curious Lives of Human Cadavers* (New York: W. W. Norton, 2003).

page 189   "Note the following examples . . ." For the manner in which the bodies of Ted Williams, Timothy Leary, and Ed Headrick were disposed, see www.infoplease.com, www.leary.com, and www.discgolfassoc.com, respectively.

page 191   "Life Gem Company of suburban Chicago . . ." For details on Life Gem Company and Eternal Reefs of Atlanta, see www.lifegem.com and www.eternalreefs.com, respectively.

page 194   "In fact, you are not human at all . . ." I have elucidated various types of dehumanization and their connection to terrorist violence in my essay "Dehumanization: Origins, Manifestations, and Remedies" in *Violence or Dialogue: Psychoanalytic Insights on Terror and Terrorism,* eds. Sverre Varvin and Vamik Volkan (London: International Psychoanalytic Association, 2003), pp. 131–145.

acknowledgments

In the course of writing this book, many "things" came to my aid. I am deeply thankful to all of them and especially to the following:

THE BUSINESS CARD of literary agent Marly Rusoff, which made it possible for me to contact her and respond to her suggestion that I write a book for a general audience. Her trust in my being able to do this, even during times when my own hope was fledgling, was of utmost importance to me, and so was the grace with which she assuaged all sorts of anxieties on my part.

THE BLUE FELT-TIP PENS AND YELLOW PADS OF PAPER that helped me write the words you have just read.

THE COMPUTER on which Katherine Ford typed the manuscript, making all sorts of alterations as we went along, with her usual cheerfulness and kindness of heart.

AMTRAK TRAINS, which helped Julia Pastore, my editor at Harmony Books, travel back and forth between New York and Philadelphia for our discussions on finetuning the manuscript. The suggestions she made for explication invariably helped my message to become clearer than it originally had been.

TELEPHONES, which helped me communicate with Shaye Areheart of Harmony Books, who offered me warm and friendly encouragement, and helped me keep in touch with Marly Rusoff, Julia Pastore, and my friends Ira Brenner, Jennifer Bonovitz, Saida Koita, and J. Anderson Thomson Jr., who listened to parts of the manuscript and gave me sound advice for its improvement.

NEW YORK'S DIWAN GRILL, where Marly and I met for lunch many times to sharpen the outline of this book during its early stages.

ACKNOWLEDGEMENTS

THE TWO DINING TABLES on which I spread all the needed material and on which I wrote the book. One of them is at my house in Ardmore, Pennsylvania, and the other is at Anju Bhargava's home in Livingston, New Jersey.

To these and many other "things," my profound thanks indeed!

index

Accidental Tourist, The (Tyler),
    66–67
Ackerman, Sol, 63
acquiring things, 17–28
    collections, 28–50
Anubis, 126
anxiety reduction, 42, 113–14,
    172–73
Arango, Ariel, 99
art collections, 34, 36
art forgeries, 144–45, 153
artificial things, 138–54
    real vs., 153–54
Aslett, Don, 171
Atta, Mohammad, 193–96

Barnes, Albert, 34
basilisk, 125
beauty, 88–90, 96–97, 99, 102–5
Best, Kimberly, 91–92
Bhatia, Pramod, 157–58
Bhatia, Supriya, 60–61
biological hybrids, 119

books, 75–76, 91–92, 174
Borges, Jorge Luis, 21, 175
Boulton, Laura, 36
Brown, Jean, 61
burial, 184, 185–86

centaurs, 124
childhood, 22–25, 26, 152
    collecting things, 43–44
    letting go of things, 39,
        167–69, 173
Chirico, Giorgio de, 61–62
circumscription, 77–78
Clean Sweep (TV show), 170, 171
clutter, 46–49
    collections vs., 30–33
    letting go of, 170–73
collections, 28, 29–50
    disposing of, 174
    of forgeries, 145–46, 149–50
    hoarding vs., 46–49
    motives for, 39–43
    value of, 31

Collins, Billy, 129, 130
Collyer brothers, 48–49
    compulsion, 32–33
Cosey, Joseph, 148–50
cosmetics, 100, 101, 107–8
counterfeits. *See* forgeries
"Creatures" (Collins), 129
cremation, 177–79, 184–85
Culp, Stephanie, 171
cultural diffusion, 132–35
cultural shifts, 108–10

Dahmer, Jeffrey, 188
Darwin, Charles, 104
Dawkins, Richard, 106
death, 27, 177–97
    meaning of, 196–97
    objects as bridge with, 64–68,
        175–76
decluttering, 170–73
dehumanization, 188–89,
    195–96
Densmore, Frances, 36
development, 21–22, 173–76
Di Bitonto, Anthony, 122
discarding things, 26–28, 170–75
    inability, 31, 39–40, 47
divinity, 78–79
divorce, 162–65
dominance, 105–6, 109

Escher, M. C., 128–29
Etcoff, Nancy, 105
Eternal Reefs, 191–92
evolutionary aesthetics, 104–8,
    114
exiles, 62–63, 165, 166–67

faith, 79
fake things, 137–54
family objects, 65–66
fertility, 105–6, 114
fetish, 100, 111–12, 113

Fletcher, Alice, 36
forgeries, 139–40, 141–52
Freud, Sigmund, 19, 29, 34, 85,
    94–95, 99, 100, 178, 180
fundamentalism, 132–35

Gandhi, Mohandas, 11–13
Ganesha, 125
Gardner, Isabella Stuart, 36
Garrison, Janet, 43–44
Geahchan, Daniel, 69
gender
    collections and, 35–36
    cultural shifts and, 108–10
    developmental stages and, 24
    nostalgia and, 72
    sexy things and, 95–110, 114
Getty, Paul, 34, 36
Gimelson, Bruce, 145–46
globalization, 132–35
Golan, Oded, 143–44
Golders Green, 177–79, 180
griffins, 124–25
Guest, Judith, 66
Guggenheim, Peggy, 36

harpy, 125
Hearst, Randolph, 29, 36
heirlooms, 28, 65
history, 85–87
hoarding, 46–49
Holocaust, 63, 189
homosexual men, 101, 109
homovestism, 113–14
hope, 75, 130
hostility, 97–98, 111–13, 114–15
humanity, 195
Hurricane Hugo, 165–66
Huxley, Julian, 23
hybrid things, 117–36

idealized past, 69–72
identity, 24, 28, 42, 173

idol worship, 80–82
Illusionless Man, The (Wheelis), 58–59
immigrants, 59–64, 166
immortality, 181, 201
inanimate hybrids, 120–23
insecurity, 31
Internet, 132, 133–34, 145–46

James ossuary, 142–44, 153
Jerusalem, 86–87
Julka, Naresh and Bubble, 32–33

Keating, Tom, 145
keepsakes, 62, 65, 67
Koncius, Jura, 170
Kovel, Terry, 29–30
Kundera, Milan, 181

Lamaire, Andre, 142–43
Leary, Timothy, 190
legendary hybrids, 123–29
Leno, Jay, 34
letting go of things, 157–76
Life Gem Company, 191
life stages, 21–28, 173–76
linking objects, 67
Live of Grime, A (TV show), 48
Long, David, 85
losing things, 159–62
loss
    collections as compensation for, 39, 40, 42, 43–44, 45
    nostalgic things and, 53–56, 57, 65–67, 72
    from traumatic event, 162–70
    See also death
Lovelace, Linda, 98

machines, hybrid, 126
Madame Tussaud's Museum, 179–80
magical powers, 157
marriage, 26, 27, 133

Marx, Karl, 37
medical uses, of body parts, 186–87
Meegeren, Hans van, 145
mementos, 62, 65, 67
memories
    collections and, 41–42
    immigrants and, 59–64
    immortality as, 181
men. *See* gender
mental death, 196
mermaids, 124
Messies Anonymous, 171
Michelangelo, 89–90
middle age, 26–28, 173–74
misplacing things, 159–62
Morris, Desmond, 20, 102
mourning process, 65–68

naked males, 101
Nasser, Atiya, 39–40
National Association of Professional Organizers, 173
National Museum of Funeral History, 185
natural disasters, 165
necrophilia, 110–11, 187
Neruda, Pablo, 18–19
nostalgia by proxy, 63–64
nostalgic things, 53–74
    collections and, 41–42
    commercialization of, 70–72
Nutting, Wallace, 69–72
nymphs, 125

"Ode to Things" (Neruda), 18–19
Oedipus complex, 94–95
old age, 28, 174–75
Ordinary People (Guest), 66

passivity, 31
Pellone, Giovanni, 122–23
permanence, 40, 175–76

Playboy, 98, 101
pornography, 97–98
profane, sacred vs., 82–85
property division, 162–65
Proust, Marcel, 64–65
puberty, 24–25

Rainier, Prince, 34
religion
    burial customs, 184, 185
    forgeries, 142–43
    hybrid creatures, 125–26
    sacred things, 75–92
reproductions, 71, 141, 153
retrospective idealization, 69–70
reverence, 77
Roach, Mary, 186–87
Roberts, Helen, 36
Rockwell, Norman, 69, 70, 72
Rushdie, Salman, 87

sacred things, 75–92
    forgery of, 142–44
    profane vs., 82–85
sadomasochism, 98, 111
Sasso, Bobby, 188–89
Satanic Verses (Rushdie), 87
satyrs, 125, 127
security objects, 22–23
self-enhancement, 102–3
self-expression, 28
self-knowledge, 73–74
sentimental things, 26–27, 57,
    72–73

separation anxiety, 22, 39, 42,
    158–59, 162–64
September 11 terrorist attack,
    191, 193–96
sexy things, 93–116
Shroud of Turin, 86
signature forgery, 148–50
Smith, Elizabeth, 43–45
States Beautiful books, 71
status, 104, 105–6, 109
Stein, David, 59–60
stereotypes, 133
Stoller, Robert, 98

terrorism, 193–96
"Things" (Borges), 175
Townsend, John Marshall, 103–4
transcendence, 131
Transformers (toys), 129
transvestism, 113–14
traumatic loss, 162–70
Trebus, Edmund, 48
Tyler, Anne, 66–67

Vermeer, Jan, 153
Volkan, Vamik, 68
voyeurism, 101

Walsh, Peter, 171
Wheelis, Allen, 58–59
Williams, John Henry, 190
Williams, Ted, 189–90
Winnicott, Donald, 22–23,
    135

about the author

SALMAN AKHTAR is a professor of psychiatry at Jefferson Medical College and Scholar-in-Residence at the Inter-Act Theater Company in Philadelphia. He lectures widely and is the recipient of the *Journal of the American Psychoanalytic Association*'s Best Paper of the Year Award. Akhtar has written many books on psychiatry and psychoanalysis, including *Immigration and Identity*, the inspiration for the play *Parinday* (Birds) recently broadcast on the BBC. He has published six volumes of poetry in English and Urdu.